'The Golden Leaf'
Love Affair

Saugus, Massachusetts

JANICE K. JAROSZ

outskirts
press

'The Golden Leaf' Love Affair
Saugus, Massachusetts
All Rights Reserved.
Copyright © 2021 Janice Jarosz
v4.0

The opinions expressed in this manuscript are solely the opinions of the author and do not represent the opinions or thoughts of the publisher. The author has represented and warranted full ownership and/or legal right to publish all the materials in this book.

This book may not be reproduced, transmitted, or stored in whole or in part by any means, including graphic, electronic, or mechanical without the express written consent of the publisher except in the case of brief quotations embodied in critical articles and reviews.

Outskirts Press, Inc.
http://www.outskirtspress.com

ISBN: 978-1-9772-2708-9

Cover & interior images © 2021 Janice K. Jarosz. All rights reserved - used with permission, unless otherwise noted.

Outskirts Press and the "OP" logo are trademarks belonging to Outskirts Press, Inc.

PRINTED IN THE UNITED STATES OF AMERICA

TABLE OF CONTENTS

Dedication	i
Introduction	iii
Chapter I: Welcome to Saugus	1
Chapter II: The Bond Family	46
Chapter III: The Lasting Legacy of Charles Henry Bond	108
Chapter IV: Meet Miss Graves	121
Chapter V: Cliftondale School closed	144
Chapter VI: Memories of the Cliftondale School	173
Chapter VII: MEG Foundation celebrates 10 years!!!	183

Dedication

I dedicate this book to the late Mr. Charles D. Bond, grandson of Mr. Charles Henry Bond who, without him, the following story could never be told.

Mr. Bond and I worked together for several years compiling the history of Saugus, Cliftondale, the cigar history of Waitt and Bond, his family and the Cliftondale School, now known as the Marleah Elizabeth Graves (MEG) Building. He also served as a director on the MEG Foundation Board for several years.

In late November of 2017, I sent him an updated article for his review of our book, but never received a response. I waited several weeks thinking he may be away but, still, nothing.

Later that month, I checked on Ancestry.com and found his death announcement. "Charlie" passed away on November 7, 2017 never seeing the final story about Cliftondale and his family. I was honored when he asked me to help put his family history together and, although it's been a challenge, it has also been a labor of love.

He was a great friend, a fellow Saugonian, and a true patriot.

Special thanks also to Ben Ross, David and Ron Jarosz for their technical support and encouragement.

Note: There are many contradictions in dates and times throughout the historical information; I tried to insert the most likely and often repeated in old records and state documents.

Introduction

Chapter I

Welcome to Saugus!

Chapter II

This chapter introduces you to the Charles William Milton Bond family, the father of Charles Henry Bond. Charles Henry grew up in Saugus, MA and played a large role in the growth and prosperity of the Cliftondale hamlet of Saugus, Massachusetts. You will 'meet' his family, view his home and other properties he built in Washington, D.C.

Chapter III

Chapter III describes the building of the Bond School, many students, and the dreaded dentist office located in the building as well.

Chapter IV

Next is a presentation of the history of Marleah Elizabeth Graves, a well-known and much-loved second grade teacher at the school along with comments from many of her fellow teachers and students.

Chapter V

In 1980, the school closed making way for more modern type buildings thus regionalizing the student population. In 2007, several Saugus citizens united to develop a plan to preserve the building and bring it back to a useful purpose. For the next 12 years dozens of residents and businesses worked to reach that goal – and we did!

Chapter VI

In 2018, a celebration was held at the, now known as the Marleah E. Graves (MEG) building, marking the many achievements made in preserving one of the most beautiful and functioning buildings in the town of Saugus.

Chapter VII

MEG celebrates it's 10-year anniversary. Mr. John Smolinsky served as MC and many from the community joined with the Board for a wonderful evening.

I am confident you will enjoy the eloquent writing and storytelling of long ago as so many writers painted their remembrances with words as taking pen to paper was the only avenue of a permanent expression of thoughts. And as you read further you will learn how the many dedicated citizens of Saugus took back the school to preserve the contributions made by Mr. Charles Bond, Miss Maleah Graves and the hundreds of school children who cherished their early childhood years.

Chapter I

Welcome to Saugus

Many historians have written that Cliftondale was once known as the 'wealthy' section of Saugus. To support that premise all one needs to do today is view the beautiful homes throughout the many streets and avenues – homes that were built generations ago still standing today. The following story hopefully explains how this section of Saugus earned the reputation and respect of so many who lived and continue to live today within its boundaries.

Several reports and articles printed those many years ago present different versions of the exciting history, but I will leave it up to you, the reader, to form your own conclusions. The spelling of names may not be accurate as many were difficult to read.

The story begins at the beginning; the early settlement Saugus tracing its growth and detailing the character of a typical New England settlement. This book takes you down through generations of Saugus and Cliftondale, a 'hamlet' and home to many thriving businesses and generous families directly responsible for the legacy they left behind.

Two early articles on Saugus gives an outline of the community. In the Cliftondale articles you will learn about the Bond family, their contributions to the success of the tobacco industry and their support and love for their families, neighbors and friends.

Early map of Saugus

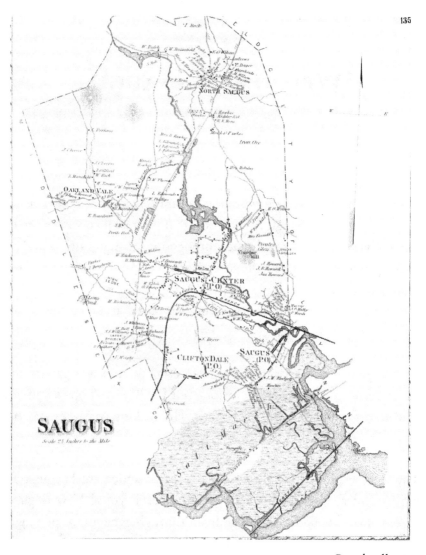

Bond collection

In 1855, Saugonian Wilbur E. Newhall, Esquire wrote the following beautiful and very detailed description of Saugus

Saugus is situated in the very southern corner of Essex County. Should you open before you a map you will notice that its general shape is a square of about twenty-three miles of each side, with its opposite corners or diagonals pointing north and south and east and west.

Saugus is an Indian name, and, as near as can be now ascertained, signifies 'extended,' separated from Massachusetts Bay by the narrow strip of land known as Revere Beach.

The Indian name of our beautiful river was 'Abousett,' and it is to be regretted that this name was ever dropped; but the white settlers fell into the custom of calling it the river at Saugus, and finally, very naturally, Saugus River, this it was when we lost the beautiful Indian name of our river.

In 1880, the population in Saugus was very near 700. And although up until 1815 our town had been mostly agricultural in its interest and pursuits, yet it was the approximate period of the increase in our manufacturing industries; shoes and woolen goods in the center of town, tobacco in Cliftondale and shoes also in East Saugus.

Saugus Centre: This brings us to the division of the town into several villages. Nature provided for these by its isolated sections of territory, suitable for farms and dwelling-houses, while separating these sections were, and still are, rocky and wooded hills, rising to no very considerable height and yet sufficient to divide our connection roads into fixed and almost necessary locations.

Round Hill is a conspicuous object and is of undoubted volcanic origin. The composition of the rock forms the hill 'Viriloid Wacke.' The base of the rock is of a pleasant green color and is filled in places with rounded nodules of quartz.

Cliftondale: Almost directly south of the Centre, and about one mile distant, is Cliftondale, formerly known as Sweetser's Corner, reached directly by Central Street alone. Recently this village has taken a wonderful start in the erection of dwelling-houses, there having been built within the past years about forty, mostly by businessmen and mechanics employed in Boston and Lynn, while some are built by speculators who hope to sell. This section already promises to be a populous portion of the town.

A large tract of land lying west of Lincoln Avenue, in Cliftondale, extending down to the Revere line, and intersected by the Saugus Branch Railroad, and now very recently bought and laid out into town lots by Charles Henry Bond, Henry Waite and E.S. Kent was formerly a noted farm. Previous to the War of 1812, John Stocker owned this farm and built himself a house.

About one-half mile south of Cliftondale, on the old traveled road which bore to the east of Lincoln Avenue as now traveled, was a famous farm of olden time, being situated partly in Saugus (then Lynn) and partly in Chelsea. The road passed between the barn and farmhouse, which stood at the foot of the hill then known as Boynton's Hill. This was the hardest hill between Salem and Boston and was much dreaded by the drivers of heavy teams. Mr. Boynton was often called upon for an extra lift, and Landlord Newhall often sent extra horses or oxen to help teams which were to stop at his tavern.

East Saugus: Coming back to the Centre again, we shall find southeasterly therefrom, about one mile distant, the village of East Saugus, situated in the river valley, and only reached by one road, now called Winter Street, on the southerly side of the valley. On account of the small area of eligible territory for building purposes, this village is compactly built, and consists principally of two streets - Chestnut Street and Lincoln Avenue – leading up from the bridge to the hill at the south of the village, where stands the village church.

Almost directly west of East Saugus is Cliftondale, one mile away and only reached by Lincoln Avenue, formerly called the old Boston Road.

Thus, we see that these three principal villages of Saugus are respectively about one mile from each other, occupying the points of an equilateral triangle, across the interior of which no road passes.

It would almost seem that this triangular district, although made up mostly of rocky hills and heretofore neglected, will, some future day, be intersected by winding avenues and dotted with beautiful hillside residences. It remains to mention two small villages of our town.

North Saugus – Some more than two miles from the Centre, and in the extreme northerly end of our township, is the village of North Saugus, a section of very excellent farming land. It is reached by Central Street, passing Prankers factory, and by the Newburyport Turnpike.

Saugus River flows beside this village, and its two tributaries, Penny Brook and Hawkes Brook flow directly through the village. These two brooks have recently been taken for a water supply by the city of Lynn; their waters have been diverted by an artificial canal and carried into Birch Pond, so called on the eastern boundary of our town.

Oaklandvale – The last village to be mentioned is Oaklandvale. This is situated a mile and a half from the Centre, northwesterly, and is only reached by the road leading to Wakefield and Melrose. This is also an agricultural district, through which flows a stream sometimes called Strawberry Brook which empties into the Saugus River below North Saugus.

The first post office was established in the village of East Saugus in 1832, with Henry Slade, Postmaster. This remained the only post office in town until 1858 when two others were established - one in Saugus Centre, Julian D. Lawrence Postmaster and Cliftondale, 1858, Wm. Williams, Postmaster.

As the population of Saugus continued to grow, several churches were built and five schools for children between the ages of five and fifteen. Businesses such as crockery ware, shoe manufacturing, farming, dairies, blacksmiths, horsehair manufacturing, apothecaries, Prankers Mills and the tobacco business – the business that put Cliftondale on the map!

Mr. Newhall continues; The growth and prosperity of the village of Cliftondale is to be traced to the manufacture of tobacco in its various forms, viz., snuff, chewing and smoking tobacco, and cigars, which had its beginning at the very close of the last century. The pioneer in this business was William Sweetser, known as William Sweetser, Jr. He manufactured snuff in a hand-mill previous to this century and sold his product principally in Salem and Marblehead.

Following close upon Mr. Sweetser was Samuel Copp. He was a native of Boston and his mother was a sister of the wife of Landlord Newhall. Having the misfortune to lose his father at an early age, he was apprenticed to a tobacconist. During his time his mother removed to Saugus and resided in the family of Landlord Newhall, where she died before he reached his majority.

On completing his apprenticeship, he at one time, repaired to Saugus and commenced a very small business, first in East Saugus then in Lynn on Boston Street near Federal Street. But after a very few years he removed to Cliftondale, built him a house and shop and married for a second time. His wife was another daughter of William Sweetser who lived close by. This was about 1807. Mr. Copp's house, with a shop a few feet west, stood on the spot now occupied by the palatial residence of Mr. Charles H. Bond.

His factory was a two-story frame building and the business then consisted mainly in the manufacture of "Fig and Pig-tail," as they were then called. The upper story was wholly devoted to hand labor and spinning "pig-tail" in the lower store were stout wooden screws in strong oaken frames, where the manufactured tobacco was pressed into boxes or keys.

In 1860, Mr. Charles Sweetser gave up the business to his two sons Charles A. and George H. who carried it on under the firm-name of Sweetser Brothers. During these years many others took up the same business, viz., Charles Raddin, who was an extensive manufacturer, also S.S. Dunn, Charles M. Bond, Silas S. Trull, Thomas F. Downing, Hiram A. Raddin and John M. Raddin.

At the beginning of the Rebellion in 1861, the cigar manufacturing practically ceased on account of the Southern market being lost and the heavy internal revenue tax placed on these low-priced goods. Pipe smoking was resorted to. The manufacture of snuff continued throughout and, since the war with little variation, until the past five years when it began to decrease.

Now, in 1887, Joseph A. Raddin, under the firm name of F.L.& J. A. Raddin, conducts the business of his father Charles, having also bought out the Sweetser Brothers' business in November 1885. Mr. Raddin's business is largely in cut smoking tobacco, some brands of which have become very popular.

The early history of Saugus/Cliftondale Massachusetts

THE BAY STATE MONTHLY

A Massachusetts Magazine. VOL. II. December 1884 No. 3

Entered according to Act of Congress, in the year 1884, by John N. McClintock and Company, in the office of the Librarian of Congress at Washington.

SKETCH OF SAUGUS.
By E. P. ROBINSON

Having somewhat minutely noticed the industries we will speak briefly of some of the dwellings. The elegant mansion and gardens of Brainerd and Henry George, Harmon Hall and Rufus A. Johnson of East Saugus, and Eli Barrett, A.A. Scott and E.E. Wilson of Saugus, C.A. Sweetser, C.H. Bond and Pliny Nickerson at Cliftondale, with their handsome lawns, rich and rare flowers and noble shade trees attract general attention. The last-mentioned estate was formerly owned by a brother of Governor William Eustis, where his Excellency used to spend a portion of his time each year.

In 1839, Mr. Charles Sweetser was elected state representative and again in 1851. Mr. Sweetser was largely engaged in the manufacture of snuff and cigars. He was a gentleman very decided in his opinions and enjoyed the confidence of the people to a large degree. (Sally Sweetser's brother).

In 1852, Mr. George H. Sweetser was the State Representative. Mr. Sweetser has also held a seat in our State Senate two years and filled various town offices. He was a prompt and energetic businessman, engaged in connection with his brother, Mr. Charles A. Sweetser, in the manufacture of snuff and cigars.

In 1867, Mr. Sebastian S. Dunn represented the District. Mr. Dunn was a dealer in snuff, cigars and spices, and is now engaged in farming in Dakota. (Charles Milton Bond's sister's husband).

Albert H. Sweetser was our last Representative, elected in 1882-3, by one of the largest majorities ever given in the District. He is a snuff manufacturer, doing business at Cliftondale, under the firm of Sweetser Bros., whom he succeeds in business. Saugus is entitled to the next Representative in 1885-6. The womb of the future will alone reveal his name.

The future of Saugus would seem to be well assured, having frequent trains to and from Boston and Lynn, with enlarged facilities for building purposes, especially at Cliftondale, where a syndicate has recently been formed, composed of Charles H. Bond, Edward S. Kent, and Henry Waite, who have purchased thirty-four acres of land, formerly belonging to the Anthony Hatch estate, which, with other adjoining lands, are to be laid out into streets and lots presenting such opportunities and facilities for building as cannot fail to attract all who are desirous of obtaining suburban residences, and thus largely add to the taxable property of Saugus and to the prosperity of this interesting locality.

(Mr. Elijah P. Robinson was born in Saugus in 1817. He served as a clerk at the Massachusetts State House retiring at 63 years old. His last address was 48 Denver Street – perhaps Robinson Street was named after him).

Village of Cliftondale of today and of yesterday
From the Lynn Item 1909

Resting quietly upon the green lawn of the broad Saugus marches, and with its head pillowed among a group of oak-covered hillocks, Cliftondale shares its graces of pleasantly located home likeness and healthful situation both with its year-round dwellers and with the passing traveler whose brief glimpse from the car window is one of lasting satisfaction.

From the distant railroad, Cliftondale, as it comes into sight - the long line of the Morton Avenue cottages leading the way. Then the church spire and the nest like collection of houses beneath and about it, and glimpses of structures on Baker hilltop still high – has a most comfortable village attractiveness, and one looks back with the desire of the explorer upon him to seek out the old houses and the new of Cliftondale the beautiful.

To take one's own time to wander through this valuable section of the town of Saugus is productive of delights the city cannot offer. The boundaries of the community are ample and the inclusive territory of a pleasing diversified nature, from the cool sunny tops of the hills to the dale like streets, broad, open and clean.

And there, as the city of Lynn has widened its limits, have come the city folks to establish as cozy and pretty homes as one may be able to find in a week's travel in the eastern part of the state.

And the Cliftondale people, themselves are cordial and agreeable. The statement of a well-known clergyman, who has been not long away from Cliftondale, and who found his efforts in the building up of his church assisted by the townsfolk in general, may well be repeated. "I never lived in a community wherein there exists such general harmony and good will and wherein the townsfolk have kept themselves on equality with one another."

The first comers to this locality bore their goods and chattels from Lynn way and Marblehead long before Cliftondale was and divided the wilderness up into a few farms of broad acres – the Sweetser's and the

Raddin's being the pioneers who, for generations, have preserved the names as well as a large portion of the properties intact.

This part of Saugus very soon became known to the traveler as Sweetser's Corner. The Raddin's and the Sweetser's were the families of note at Sweetser's Corner, and the latter nomenclature and that of Raddin's town were often used interchangeably.

The Pater families and the sons of both families were the earliest to found and engage in the business of tobacco and snuff manufacture, and at one time, the section was known thereby as the growing town of Lynn because of its shoemaking.

There were snuff takers in about all the families of those days and the business of the preparation of snuff was a profitable one, many of the villagers following the trade of the Sweetser's and the Raddin's. Lynn has flourished in its shoe business, but the Sweetser's Corner snuff makers have all gone the way of most of the snuff takers, only a portion of the old factories and a few of the memories of the manufacturers remaining to tell the tale.

Today but a single manufacturer of novelties for the holidays has a concern of leading importance here, though the enterprising Cliftondale businessmen are keeping the town booming right along as they perceive the everyday needs of the people, their well-appointed shops notably those of Merchants row, adorning the square, and giving activity to the side streets.

Cliftondale is numbered Precinct 2 in the town of Saugus. J. Arthur Raddin, one of the town fathers, being the chairman of the towns Board of Selectmen. This precinct has an approximate valuation of $2,000,000 and with a population of between 2,500 and 3,000.

The most remarkable growth has been noted during the past decade, during which time a number of new avenues have been opened up and scores of houses have been erected thereon. A number of the former waste places on the adjoining hills have been made habitable and are now adorned with many fine, modern residences. The precinct has three mixed schools The Cliftondale, the Lincoln Avenue, and the Felton Schools, and there are three churches; the Methodist, the Congregational and the Pentecostal. The Methodist Church is almost one with the history of the section.

The town fathers are making strenuous efforts to get rid of the mosquito pest and the people are hoping for an appropriation to be applied in the draining of the stagnant pools on the marshes. Many of the pools on the marshes are clogged up and here the mosquitoes have their habitation to the regret of the Cliftondale people and Saugus in general.

The post office has been in existence for the past 75 years. John Trull was the first postmaster and he was followed in that capacity by Mrs. Maria Putnam. The present incumbent, Miss M. E. Fiske, has held the position for the past 25 years.

Among the prominent townsmen who live here, and who represent the town in the Legislature and in its general business may be mentioned the following:

Representative James B. Holliday, Herbert M. Forestall, Representative 1907-1908; Ernest Nocera, assessor of the town; Anthony Hatch, Superintendent of Streets; Henry F. Fiske, Selectman; J. Arthur Raddin, Chairman of the Saugus Board of Selectmen; Alvah Sheppard, member of the School Committee; Robert T. Allen, member of the Water Board; Judge William E. Ludden, trial Justice of Saugus; Chas. Woodbridge, Crawford Stocker, Arthur B. Smith, A.B. Coates, and Charles O Thompson, Chief of Police.

Patriotic Sons Were Ever Ready

Saugus Is Well Represented Among Men at Lexington and Bunker Hill

MARKER AT GRAVES KEEP MEMORY GREEN

Lynn Item September 4, 1909

The patriotism of this good old town has been evidenced in every struggle for right. An Item report in casting about for data regarding the part played by Saugus in the Revolutionary War did discover no more valuable or authentic article relating thereto than the complete and scholarly paper long ago read at a public gathering by Horace H. Atherton, Jr., whose research and study have placed him about the most exact and interesting of local historians. Mr. Atherton thus writes of the patriots:

Saugus sent men to the village green at Lexington, furnished more than its quota of patriots for the battle of Bunker Hill and its soldiers fought with conspicuous bravery all through with those trying days of the Republic's infancy. The Saugus Company of Minute Men was the largest of the five companies from Lynn at the fight of April 19, 1775.

In it were 61 men, mostly farmers. They were led by the redoubtable David Parker, who marched them over the road from Saugus to Lexington. In those days the distance was about 40 miles and the route taken was up through Malden.

This hard band of citizen soldiers was Saugus men, whose names follow, together with those of 38 others, who served during the later periods of the war:

"Lemuel Allen, John Batts, Thomas Henry, Aaron Boardman, Ivory Boardman, Amos Boardman, Samuel Boardman, William Boardman,

Nathaniel Boynton, Samuel Breeden, Benjamin Brown, Rufus Brown, Israel Burrill, John Burrill, Abner Cheever, Abner Cheever, Jr, Alijah Cheever, John Cheever, Stephen Coates, Phillip Coates, William Coates, Joshua Danforth, Joseph Eaton, Joseph Edmunds, Jonathan Felt, Joseph Felt, Joshua Felt, Charles Florence, Thomas Florence, David Fuller, Peter Fuller, Benjamin Goldthwaite, Moses Hart, Adam Hawkes, Elhanan Hawkes, Nathan Hawkes, Thomas Hawkes, Richard Hill, Robert Hill, William Hill, Alijah Hitchings, Daniel Hitchings, John Hitchings, Nathaniel Hitchings, Thomas Hitchings, William Hitchings, Ezekiel Howard, Joshua Howard, Timothy Hutchinson, Benjamin Jacobs, Ebenezer Lethe, Amos Leeds, James Lelah, Benjamin Mansfield, Samuel Mansfield, Thomas Mansfield, James Marble, Josiah Martin, David Newman, Thomas Newman, Calvin Newhall, David Parker, John Pool, Amos Pratt, Benjamin Raddin, Samuel Rhodes, Henry Roby, Rev. Joseph Roby, Thomas Roby, Ebenezer Stocker, Thomas Stocker, Ephraim Stocker, E. Stocker Jr., Enoch Stocker, John Symmes, Francis Smith, Francis Smith, Jr., Ebenezer Stacey, Phineas Sweetser, Samuel Sweetser, Amos Porter, Richard Tuttle, Benjamin Twist, Nathaniel Veal, Samuel Veal, Benjamin Wilson, Samuel Wilson, Jr., Ezra Waitt.

David Parker's bravery at Lexington led to his promotion as major. He was born in Saugus, May 30, 1734. He served in the Burgoyne campaign, and was in the battles of Stillwater and Saratoga.

John Boardman was ploughing in the field when the call came. He barely had time to tell his brother William and to bid his mother goodbye when he was taken prisoner on board the prison ship Jersey where he was poisoned.

And so on, through a long and glowing list of true patriots, every man of who had an honorable and commendable career.

Joseph Eaton Recalled

At the exercise commemorative of the soldiers of the Revolution from Saugus, held in the Town Hall, Monday, June 18, 1906, under the auspices of the Lynn Historical Society, the town of Saugus, old Essex Chapter, S.A. R. Chapter of the Third Plantation, D.R. and kindred organizations, Horace H. Atherton, Jr, of Saugus, who presided, said in part:

"It seems eminently fitting that these exercises should be held on the 131st anniversary of the Battle of Bunker Hill, in which at least one Saugus man, Joseph Eaton, is known to have been an actual participant. As many as five other Saugus men, Thomas Berry, Amos Boardman, Ezra Brown, Israel Burrell and Thomas Hutchinson, were in the immediate vicinity with their regiments, and Amos Boardman was really in the latter part of the action.

Thomas Berry, Ezra Brown, Israel Burrell and Thomas Hutchinson were at what was then called Cobble Hill.

Each and every one of these six Saugus men did his duty where he found himself assigned. Saugus should feel proud of the fact that at this late day, when the records are so dim and incomplete, it can be substantiated beyond reasonable doubt that six of her sons directly or indirectly took part in one of the bloodiest battles of all history, where, in an hour and a half, the number of killed and wounded was more than 30 per cent of the men engaged.

Joseph Eaton enlisted in 1775 in June, in Hart's company, Col. Thomas Gardner's 37th regiment, and was a corporal.

So much was Saugus at Bunker Hill 131 years ago today. Now as to Saugus, Lexington and Concord. What we designate in these days as the Saugus Company of Minutemen was the largest of the five men, mostly farmers commanded by Maj. David Parker. They marched over the road to Lexington and Concord on the memorable 19th of April 1775 and did heroic service in the country's cause.

Later, some 38 men from Saugus enlisted in the Continental Army, thus making a total of 99 men whose memories we honor today. The graves of nearly 40 of them are in yonder cemetery; one lies at Riverside; several sleep their last sleep at Lynn, and the remainder are not unhonored nor unsung, even though some rest in unknown graves."

Mr. Atherton has in his possession a photographic copy of the commission of Jonathan Brown, of Saugus, who saw service in the Revolutionary War. Jonathan Brown, private, son of Ephraim and Anna (Twist) was born in Saugus Sept. 22, 1755. With his brothers Ephraim and Ezra, he marched with his company to Monotony and was in the "runaway fight of the regulars."

In 1776, he removed to Salem, where he soon afterward married. He enlisted in February 1776, in Captain Benjamin Epee's' Company, Col. Smith's regiment, and served until Boston was evacuated by the British entering the town with his Company.

In the fall of that year he served as Sergeant in Captain Nathan Sergeant's Company, Col. Jacob Gerrish's Regiment of guards. Upon the arrival of General Burgoyne and his army of prisoners at Cambridge, his company did guard duty of them for six months. He entered the service January 26, 1779, as Second Lieutenant of the same company and served until May 7, doing duty under Major Gates around Boston.

In 1780, he enlisted in Captain Stephen Webb's Company and served 18 months in a fort near Salem. He was borne on the rolls of the Continental Army as late as Oct. 28, 1783, where he appears on a pay warrant of Captain Webb's Company. Mr. Brown is probably buried in Salem, but the spot is unknown.

Revolutionary men of Sweetser's Corner

It was nine o'clock at night on the nineteenth of April 1775, when the courier bearing the news of the fight at Lexington reached Saugus from Malden. The word spread rapidly throughout the town, it having first been known at Cliftondale. A horseman flew to the tavern and the alarm was sounded throughout the countryside. Not a moment was wasted, and before midnight the first detachment of Minute Men, including several from Cliftondale, was galloping over the road, then known as the county street running from Boston to Salem, and which went, as now, by the way of Malden, but along a different route back of Baker's Hill.

There were five companies which went to Lexington and Concord from what is now the separated sections of the old town of Lynn, and the so-called Saugus Company, that is the one which was recruited from what at present includes the territorial limits of the town, was the largest of the five. This company was drilled in the old Landlord Newhall's Tavern at East Saugus.

It met at irregular intervals, and its guiding hands were Major David Parker, its commander, Parson Roby and, doubtless, others. Parker conducted a blacksmith's shop on the so-called county road not far from the tavern. The patriotic citizens of what is now Saugus gathered here, and, in the large room before the open fireplace, discussed the pressing theme of the time, which was whether or not the mother country would force the colonies to armed resistance against the crown.

David Parker was born in 1744 and died in 1810 at Malden. He is buried in the old Bell Rock Cemetery. His grave, near the wall, on the north side, is under a spreading maple, and is marked with a slate stone. The Saugus Branch trains on the Boston & Maine skirt along this cemetery at Bell Rock Station. In addition to these sixty-three men from Saugus who answered the first call to arms, there were thirty-eight others who served during the later periods of the war.

Among those from what is now the Cliftondale section of the town were Nathaniel Boynton; Benjamin, Ezra, Ephraim, Rufus and Jonathan Brown, father and sons. Jonathan Brown was a second lieutenant, the three Cheever's, Abner, Abner, Jr., and John; three Coates's, Stephen, Philip, and William; Joshua Danforth and Joseph Eaton. Eaton was at Bunker Hill and so were five other Saugus men, including two from Cliftondale. Their names were Thomas Berry, Amos Boardman, Ezra Brown, Israel Burrell and Thomas Hutchinson. Eaton and Brown were Cliftondalers.

Saugus should feel proud of the fact that at this late day, when the records are so dim and incomplete, it can be substantiated that at least six Saugus men directly took part in this famous battle, one of the bloodiest of all history, up to that time; where in an hour and a half the number killed and wounded was more than thirty per cent, of the men engaged.

Other Cliftondalers in the Revolutionary War were the Stockers, Ebenezer, his son, Ebenezer, Jr., Elijah, Enoch, Ephraim, and Thomas; the Sweetser's, Phineas and Samuel; Ben Bullard Raddin, ancestor of former Selectman J. Arthur Raddin, and Lemuel Allen, who was a sergeant in the Saugus Company. Allen married Parson Roby's daughter, and lived on what was later known as the George N. Miller place, northwest of the Cliftondale Depot. He held the highly honorable position of hog reeve and warden in 1766, 1769 and 1781.

Walker's map of Cliftondale 1882

Bond collection

Jackson Street

Bond collection

Alfred A. Ferguson Apothecary

Left to right: Dr. Perkins, Alfred M. Ferguson,
H.W. Butler, unnamed.

Bond Collection

How Cliftondale Got its Name

(Article taken from the Lynn Item August 21, 1909)

"There have been changes enough to interest me in the growth of Cliftondale during the past 40 years, so many that I had not dreamed of when I used to see but a half-dozen houses. In sight of my own house," remarked one of the cheeriest and happiest of the aged resident, Mrs. Mary Roache at her home on Central Street to a reporter from the Item, as she welcomed him the other day.

"I was born but a half mile from here, East Saugus way, when the Sweetser's and the Raddin's were the leading ones in this part of town. If I live until June 12, 1910, I shall have reached the age of 80 and my outlook upon life is very bright and still for the peace that I possess, and that has always been mine. New neighbors and new friends have come through all these years, and the little town has grown up about me.

I welcome the changes and the newcomers, but I miss the former associations of Cliftondale of some years ago. As I look from my window, I recollect how the old Danforth house, old even then, looked as it stood alone but a few rods away on this side of the road. Across the way stood an old pottery building, one of the first to be erected in Saugus, and just beyond stood the Downing house and the old Methodist Church. This side stood the little old schoolhouse, where the men and women for generations went to school."

Old Danforth House

Bond collection

Sweetser's Corner. This place was called when I was young, and the business of the place was that of snuff and tobacco manufacture. Charles Sweetser was the proprietor of the snuff and tobacco factory, and he was assisted by his sons, George, Henry and Augustus, the former being the well-known representative of the town.

I believe it used to be told that just as the first railroad was about to be run through the town, there was a sort of controversy as to the name it should be called. It was somehow left to the decision of two sisters, the Misses Kidder, manufacturers of Kidders' Cordial, very well-known in those times. The tradition runs that one of the sisters said, "Let's call the town Cliff, as it stands beneath a cliff."

But the other said: "Why might it not be named Dale, as it surely is in a sort of dale or valley, beneath the hills?" They united their opinions, finally, and agreed that Cliftondale would be the best.

How Cliftondale got its name

Woman wins $10 Prize

Mrs. Roache is often called the mother of the Methodist Church in Cliftondale and she is the friend of the people of all denominations. Her father was Thomas Newhall and her mother, Mary Parker, was the daughter of the brave Major Parker, who was the leader of the Saugus Company at the battle of Lexington. He lived at East Saugus and was a blacksmith by trade. Mrs. Roaches' grandfather, Joseph Stocker Newhall, lived in the old house on the East Saugus end, which still stands and whose early history is but little known.

Across from the house stood four old elms and beneath these (George) Washington and his suite rested, while on their way to Salem, Mrs. Roaches' grandmother bringing them refreshments of glasses of milk.

Lafayette also stopped under these same old elms as he passed through the town.

(Editor's note: The milk given to George Washington is of a questionable nature as other reports state a mug of rum was the drink of choice.)

Cliftondale Square

Dwelling Places of Early Settlers

Taken from the Lynn Item, August 21, 1909

Sentinels and guardians of the traditions of other days. Cliftondale's old houses preserve a more than passing interest for both townsman and traveler. They are the milestones of the town's history, and beneath their gray roofs have been established the rendezvous of man a locally historic pilgrimage.

Sad to relate though, descendants of the former inhabitants of the old homes have been somewhat lax in the keeping of the old records and few Sweetser's Corner homes may refer to its consecutive history of any of the houses, off-hand.

The picture of the old Anthony Hatch house, which appears in the Item with this article, has never before found its way into print. The rooftree was one of the landmarks of the section. The centre of the Cliftondale Square, at the present time, has a totally different appearance from that when the Hatch house stood there.

There still are the century-old elms rising majestically over the greensward in the centre of the square. Beneath them once stood the Hatch house, fronting on Lincoln Avenue, but now passed along with the building of the street in the rear.

The old house was once known as the Boynton Farm, the latter one of the largest in the vicinity extending through the present Franklin Park. In the year 1847, Anthony Hatch, who hailed from Medford, came here and bought the place of Robert Carlton, which was then known to have been over 100 years old.

Cliftondale Rotary

Bond collection

Mr. Hatch was made Road Commissioner of the town and became a prominent farmer and took many prizes at the hands of the Horticultural Society in Boston, of which he was a member of a committee on vegetables.

The old home was removed from this locality in 1865 and is now at the end of Laurel Street, where it is occupied by Anthony Hatch 3rd, and Anthony Hatch 4th.

Bond Block from Lincoln Square, Cliftondale, Mass

Bond collection

Saugus Tobacco Industry Flourished for 150 years

Saugus Tobacco Industry Flourished for 150 Years

Saugus Herald - Feb 2, 1940

Civil War Marked End of Once Lucrative Business Which Employed Many Here

A hundred years ago Cliftondale, which is now so largely residential in character, was well-known under the name of Sweetser's Corner as a manufacturing center. The products which carried its fame of the little community all over the country were chocolate and snuff. Probably it would be hard today to find anyone in Saugus who uses, or perhaps has even seen, the second of these two commodities, yet the history of its manufacture and marketing is an interesting and important chapter in the development of our town. Before the Civil War only one factory in America, that of the Lorrillard company in New York City, had a larger plant for the making of snuff than the etsablishment on Lincoln street in Saugus. From Canada to the Gulf, the scented tobacco ground beside the Saugus river was a favorite and familiar ware.

Tobacco and its products early appear in Saugus records. The annals of the town mention them first with horror and distaste, for an order in 1632 made it a punishable offence to "take tobacco" in public ("to take" evidently meaning "to use" rather than to harvest or steal, both of which offences are still current) and fixing a fine of a penny for each conviction. In 1638 the elders of the colony so far relented as to permit a man on a journey to smoke when he was five miles from any habitation, provided that no one was injured by the act and the woods were not set on fire. For such reprobates as neglect to take themselves five miles into the wilderness before lighting a peaceful pipe, the fine was ten shillings. Thereafter the habit of "taking tobacco" seems to have grown unchecked, until in 1794 George Makepeace, at his mill on the Saugus river, hollowed out a couple of button-wood logs for mortars and began to grind tobacco. Thus began the snuff-making industry in Saugus.

CIGARS AND SNUFF

The first Sweetser made cigars and snuff over a shop bearing the agreeably exotic sign, "West India Goods," early in the seventeenth century. Other men whose names were to become important in the tobacco industry gathered about the "Corner," notably Copp, Raddin, Danforth, Trull and the still flourishing Waitt and Bond. At length, in the forties, the Sweetser factory employed some fifty persons, altogether, and the product commanded a countrywide sale.

Since the habit of snuff-taking has all but died out in this part of America, there are no doubt many people hereabouts who have never encountered a sample of this delicate form of processed tobacco. Of all the methods of preparing the leaf, snuff-making is the most difficult, complex, and lengthy. Probably the early colonists, returning to Europe with the tobacco plant, reported that the Indians not only smoked the dried leaf, but also ground and inhaled it. By the middle of the eighteenth century this latter form of "tobacco-taking" had become by far the most universally popular. Probably snuff gained its wide usage because its pleasantly perfumed dust was more agreeable in a lady's salon than the heavy smoke of a cigar, and indeed smoking in a drawingroom was, until almost the present day, regarded as very bad form.

To make the most costly form of snuff requires from eighteen to twenty months. The tobacco is first moistened with salt water, as a preservative, and then packed into cakes, which are sliced and stored for five or six months to ferment. Next comes grinding, and thereafter another ten months of storage, at a temperature of 100 to 130 degrees Fahrenheit. Some fragrant essence, such as lavender, orange flower oil, bergamot, clove, attar of roses, tonquin-bean, jasmine or musk, is then added, and the snuff matured for another month. The ingredient added to the tobacco determines the flavor and scent of the snuff, and formulas were jealously guarded as trade secrets. By the time the process is complete, about two thirds of the nicotine and most of the malic and citric acids of the tobacco are disappeared. Sometimes, in order to increase the slightly acrid sensation which was the special quality of snuff, a little quick-lime was used in curing the tobacco. This drier type of snuff was known as Scotch snuff, and it was principally this sort which was made in Saugus.

USE OF SNUFF

The use of snuff was so general that as many accessories were made to go with it as are found today for cigarettes. For users of the type of snuff which was sold unground were made hand graters. Some were tiny affairs of carved ivory, to carry in a pocket, and others, known as mulls, stood upon tables and were generally made of a silver-mounted ram's head. For the still more usual snuff which came ready ground, jewellers made boxes of precious metals and enamel, often ornamented with jewels and family crests. In European courts the most frequent mark of royal favor was the gift of a suitably ingraved snuff-box, and even after the habit fell into comparative disuse, sovereigns continued to present gemmed snuff-boxes instead of decorations to visiting diplomats.

But the habit of snuff-taking, though we think of it principally in connection with the Court of France before the Revolution, or

Bo

Tobacco Industry article continued

Dr. Johnson's circle of wits and writers in London, was by no means confined to Europe or to cosmopolitan company. Boxes made of horn or tortoise-shell were often tucked into the pockets of a pioneer's jeans or an Indian-hunter's buckskins. Traders in prairie-schooners and Yankee pedlars with their wide-roving, jingling buggies carried kegs of Saugus snuff along with powder-horns and bowie knives. A coarse grade of snuff, made of the stems and inferior leaves of the plant and cured more rapidly than the better sort, was popular among the slaves of the southern plantations, and such snuff is still used in the rural sections of the south today. Indeed, the trademark of Mackaboy Snuff, made in Saugus, was so familiar in the south and west that for many years after the factory had ceased to operate, orders continued to come in from these territories.

After the Civil War snuff began to decline in popularity, either because of its costly and difficult manufacture or because of the widening use of cigarettes. Saugus, cut off by the War from the southern tobacco crops and burdened with internal revenue taxes, ceased to grind the leaves. Today about twenty thousand tons of snuff are made and marketed in the United States, and some nine hundred tons in the British Isles, though in France, where the habit is by no means extinct, the manufacture of snuff is important enough to be under government control. But in Saugus there remain only memories of the trade which once scented the winds along the Saugus river and helped to build up the prosperity of our town.

Bond Collection

House Stood for 350 Years

The Old Bond House.

Bond Collection

When Charles Milton Bond removed with his family from Hampstead, N.H. and bought the old place, now no longer in existence, and well-known as the Bond house to later generations, he reckoned that the place was 206 years old, and it was from that time on in the hands of the Bond family for 150 years. The picture herewith given is a good representation of the house painted by a local artist.

Saugus Tobacco Capital of Nation in Early Day

Taken from the Lynn Item, April 8, 1947 and written by Paul A. Haley

"Segar" and Snuff Manufactured by Many in Latter Part of 1800's

Crippled from birth, a teen-age boy founded a great tobacco dynasty in Cliftondale during the Civil War.

Anxious to help his widowed mother after the father had died a hero on a Southern battlefield, Henry Waite started in the cellar of his home in North Revere, just over the Saugus Line, the cigar business which made the name of Waite & Bond famous throughout the United States.

Inflation gripped the nation; and flour was selling at $75.00 per barrel. A woman grieving over the loss of her husband and with a hungry family to support was distracted. "I'll earn a barrel of flour rolling cigars," said young Waite, and on this humble foundation was erected a business which became known from coast to coast.

(Courtesy of Lynn Item)

The famous J.A. Cigar

For generations the product of the firms 'J.A's have been known where good cigars have been esteemed, and the firm, long since moved from Saugus, is today the last relic of a thriving business which in the latter years of the last century stamped Saugus as the "Winston-Salem of the North." Just as the famed southern city is today the center of the cigarette business, Saugus and particularly the Cliftondale section, was the most famous spot in the United States for the manufacture of cigars and snuff.

Saugus "segars" were known from coast to coast in our great-grandfather's days, and Charles H. Bond, founded with Waite, the great tobacco house of Waite and Bond and built one of the finest mansions in Greater Lynn on the site of the present Cliftondale Methodist Church with the lush profits of the business.

Many Identified with Business

Waite and Bond, however, were merely the most successful of a large number of Saugus and Cliftondale cigar manufactures who flocked into that community from abroad shortly after Samuel

Copp started the first factory on what is now Mountain Avenue, Cliftondale, in 1809.

It was from one of the most successful tobacco families, the Sweetser's, that the name of Sweetser Junior High School was taken, and Cliftondale Square, until comparatively recent days, was known as 'Sweetser's Corner.' It bore this title when General George Washington rode through the square in his chariot in 1787 a few months before assuming the office of President of the United States and was known by the same name in 1828 when Lafayette was the guest of the city of Lynn, MA.

Mr. Copp founded the tobacco business in 1809 and as recently as 1878 there were 36 people in Cliftondale engaged in the cigar business and listed in the "Massachusetts Gazetteer" of that year. Many of them, however, were in business in a small way, traveling a route through Lynn, Peabody, Danvers, Topsfield, and Lynnfield, leaving the tobacco to be rolled into 'segars' and calling the following week for the finished product. Others employed girls from nearby farms to roll the cigars in crude Saugus factories. The cigars were then packaged and taken to Boston to be sold.

While Cliftondale specialized in the 'segar' business with such figures as the Sweetser's, Raddin's, and other controlling the traffic, East Saugus was equally known as the greatest snuff center of New England. At the East Saugus Bridge during the greater part of the 19th century stood the snuff mill which handled the greatest volume of this product in the nation.

Waite and Bond prospered, perhaps to a greater extent than their competitors, and Henry Waite later donated to the town of Revere the land in Franklin Park across the street from his home where now stands the Henry Waite School named in his honor.

The Methodist Church

Bond collection

The first Methodist building was built on a lot of land given by Charles Sweetser, on the southerly side of Lincoln Avenue near St. Margaret's Church. Here the congregation worshipped from 1858 until a disastrous blaze of June 19, 1914 which leveled the church.

The Bond Mansion

Bond collection

The 'Bond" Mansion,' was a large, three-story mansard roof house built in the 1860's by George Henry Sweetser. It was said to be one of the first houses in the country in which electric wiring was installed. Much of the land in the area had long been in the possession of the Sweetser family.

An interesting picture of Cliftondale as it was in 1884 is contained in an old atlas of Essex County in the possession of the writer. It contains maps of Cliftondale, Saugus Center, and East Saugus, as they were in those days and gives a picture of the community far removed from the present pleasant, residential communities and busy Cliftondale Square.

In 1884, the farm of Anthony Hatch comprised the greater part of Cliftondale Square The owner had just died after being gored to death by a bull and the great farm, stretching from the present square to the Franklin Park line and down Essex Street to the railroad station, was about to be divided.

Two sons, Anthony and James, decided to sell off the greater part of their boundless acres for home development, and to move the old home to where it now stands at the extreme end of Laurel Street. James took the part of the farm which he operated until his recent death on Eustis Street, and Anthony assumed control of the present farm operated today by his son-in-law George J. Caddy.

The Hatch house and barns then stood directly where the green is in Cliftondale Square. At the present Butler Drug Company at the corner of Jackson Street, Bond operated his cigar business and where the present Walkey's Block is, A.H. Sweetser had his snuff manufactory.

E. O. Copp's cigar plant was on nearby Mountain Avenue where the present Davis News Store is and was also the cigar manufacturing plant of C. A. Sweetser. Mr. Trull employed some 50 girls at his plant where Dr. Leroy C. Furbush now resides.

Cigars built this mansion

First YMCA On Present Site

The cornerstone for the magnificent new church property was laid on June 5, 1915, and it was dedicated on March 5, 1916, by Bishop John W. Hamilton. In more recent years the handsome Community House adjoining the property was constructed during the pastorate of the late Rev. Arthur A. Pitman.

An interesting fact is that the old Bond mansion just prior to its loss by fire housed in its coach house a Saugus YMCA. The coach house stood on the exact site of the present Community House where a YMCA is now in operation with the co-operation of the Lynn organization.

The old map of Cliftondale is revealing. It shows that the post office then stood on the site of the present hall of Saugus Council, Knights of Columbus, on Jackson Street. The previous building on this site—the first Post Office in Saugus—and one of the oldest buildings in the town—is the home on Granite Court formerly owned by Charles Bateman. Operated by Martha Fiske—the town's first postmistress—it was moved to Granite Court as the first house on the street.

Essex Street, going out of Cliftondale Square, was then known as Boston Street. The only building in 1884 until one reached the corner of what is now Eustis Street was the property of the Hatch family and is still occupied by Mrs. Elsie Wadsworth, daughter of Mr. and Mrs. James Hatch. The land now occupied by the Cliftondale Congregational Church, the Cliftondale School, the Church of the Nazarene and all of the houses now standing there, was at that time merely vacant pasturage of the Hatch farm.

The situation was not unusual, for the greater part of the now thriving community of Cliftondale was also farmland and part of the extensive holdings of the Hatch family. All of the land on the westerly side of Lincoln Avenue from Cliftondale Square to the Franklin Park line was then farmland. A dozen attractive streets and several hundred homes were built after the property was opened for development in the next few years.

Proceeding down Essex Street toward West Cliftondale, there were virtually no homes in those days until one reached the crossing of the Eastern Railroad, now the Saugus branch of the Boston and Maine Railroad where the home of W. M. Stocker stood. This typically New England structure, built in 1847 as the date on the walls in the attic attests, was in the hands of the Stocker family until recently, when it was acquired by Leslie E. Parsons, Jr., of the Parsons Fuel Company.

CIGARS BUILT THIS MANSION on the site of the present Cliftondale Methodist Church in the days when Saugus was the "Winston-Salem of the North." Charles H. Bond of the famed Waite & Bond Cigar Company was one of the many Saugus people engaged in the tobacco business in the last century.

Well-known citizens of Saugus, Massachusetts

CHARLES SWEETSER,
First of the Name to Manufacture Cigars and Snuff in Cliftondale.

CHARLES AUGUSTUS SWEETSER,
Famous Snuff and Cigar Manufacturer of Cliftondale.

CHARLES RADDIN,
Who Manufactured Tobacco Goods in Cliftondale Nearly 100 Years Ago.

CHARLES MILTON BOND,
Founder of the Bond Cigar Business.

MRS. AUGUSTA RADDIN,
Eighty-Year-Old Resident.

MRS. MARY ROACHE,
One of Cliftondale's Oldest Residents.

J. ARTHUR RADDIN,
Chairman of the Saugus Board of Selectmen.

HENRY F. FISKE,
Selectman.

HON. JAMES B. HALLIDAY,
Member of House of Representatives

Bond collection

CLIFTONDALE

By Horace T. Atherton 1915

Cliftondale may well be said to be the new part of Saugus, new in the sense that it has developed in the later years. Its growth has been rapid, substantial, and gratifying. In the old days it was known as "Sweetser's Corner," and in that period, was the location of important activities in the tobacco and allied trades. There were a few scattered houses there in the Revolutionary period, but Cliftondale did not put on its seven league boots until about 1800.

Snuff was the particular form of the weed that was the cornerstone of its mercantile life and the vehicle which rolled it into prominence. William Sweetser, Jr., made it by hand previously and disposed of it "up county," as he wrote. In his footsteps came Samuel Copp, a native of Boston, whose establishment became the second building at "Sweetser's Corner," in the square. If Samuel Copp could revisit Cliftondale Square during our present celebration he would be justified in lifting his eyebrows at the progress and development which has occurred in a little more than one hundred years in the vicinity of his snuff mill, whose only music in his time was its grinding mortars.

Charles Sweetser, in 1820, appeared on the scene and bought out Copp. Sweetser added the manufacture of "short sixes" and "long nines" to the business, "two-firs" as they were sometimes designated. They sold readily, and Sweetser, who was a son of William, developed and cultivated the trade very successfully. His wares were sold all over the United States and British provinces without the aid of pictures of baseball players, premiums and other catch-penny schemes which modern efficiency has produced for the tobacco industry. He retired in 1860 and was succeeded by his two sons, Charles A. and George H.

Sweetser, both of whom are remembered by the present generation, and some of whose descendants still live in Cliftondale.

Others entered the same line of business endeavor at the "Corner," among them Charles Raddin, S, S. Dunn, Charles M. Bond, Silas S. Trull, Thomas F. Downing, Hiram A. Raddin, and John M. Raddin.

The war of 1861 practically ended the cigar business of "Sweetser's Corner," owing to the loss of the southern tobacco market and the heavy internal revenue taxes placed on these low-priced goods. The business thereafter decreased gradually but steadily from year to year, until now, so far as the writer knows, it is entirely extinct in Saugus, although two old families of this section, Revere and Saugus, are represented in the well-known firm of Waitt & Bond, who do a large and successful cigar business in Boston.

It had its inception at Cliftondale, where Mr. Bond's father was for years engaged in it. Henry Waitt and Charles H. Bond, both deceased, are well remembered in Saugus, the latter as one of our most highly respected residents and the former as a citizen of Revere, just over the line from Saugus. The public school in that portion of Revere, known as Franklin Park, is named the Henry Waitt School, and Charles H. Bond's generosity in connection with the Saugus public schools and the Cliftondale Congregational Church are recalled with gratitude by members of the present generation.

Jackson's Meadow, on what is now Central Street (built 1837), from Cliftondale to Saugus Centre, contained a peat deposit and some fine blue clay. About 1808, William Jackson, an Englishman, and for whom, we assume, Jackson Street is named, bought a farm in this part of the town, and finding this clay adapted for brown and red earthenware, began its manufacture, which he continued for four years, Wilbur F. Newhall informs us.

In 1853, Kent's curled hair industry started at Cliftondale. Enoch T. Kent was its pioneer, living in that section. In 1866 he went to the Centre and established a factory on Shute's Brook, near the railroad station.

Cliftondale has the Felton School, named for Cornelius Conway Felton. The history of the arrival of the Felton's in Cliftondale is interesting. When the Newburyport Turnpike was projected, tolls were exacted from its travelers. The proprietors dispatched Cornelius Felton of Newburyport to collect them at Saugus, and Hawkes tells us of "the little toll house" (gate No. 1), where the elder Felton performed that important service.

His eldest son, Cornelius Conway Felton, was then a mere child. Hawkes continues:

The story of the efforts of the toll keeper's son to obtain the rudiments of an education will long be related in Saugus, but of the boy who became the profound Greek scholar and President of Harvard, his biographer. Rev. A. P. Peabody, D.D., says:

"Mr. Felton filled a very large and, in some respects, a unique place in our world of letters. It is seldom that an adept in one department is a proficient in all the essential branches of liberal culture. This was, however, true of him. While as a classical scholar he had no superior, he was versed in the languages and familiar with the best literature of modern Europe, was largely conversant with national science, and had a highly educated and nicely critical taste in the entire realm of art.

The ability that he showed in many and diverse directions, had its scope been narrower, would have been accounted as genius of a very high order; but its breadth and versatility was more than genius. Within the largest bounds of a liberal education no demand was made upon him that found him incapable or unprepared: and whatever he did he did so well that he seemed to have a special adaption for it."

Felton Street is named for this distinguished family, some of whom are buried in the old cemetery at the Centre.

The Tudor Home

Bond collection

Cliftondale suggests the country house of Col. William Tudor, "Rockwood," is now the Saugus Town Home. William Tudor was a Revolutionary officer and a friend of General Washington. In 1805, his third son, Frederic Tudor, evolved a scheme of harvesting and marketing ice.

The plans seemed feasible and, in that year, he had cut from a pond in front of his father's country place on the Turnpike a large quantity of ice, which he loaded on a schooner and shipped to Martinique. He accompanied the cargo, although laughed at by his associates and neighbors, who pronounced him mentally unbalanced. Tradition informs us that the consignees of the ice were unappreciative of its value, but the fact remains that the foundation of a Saugus industry is thus chronicled.

Rockwood was purchased by the town in 1823 for the almshouse, a designation later very appropriately changed to Saugus Home, at the suggestion of the late George G. Spur, whose ideas were subsequently ratified by a vote in town meeting.

Another one of the distinguished houses of old Cliftondale is the Dr. Cheever place, on what is now Essex Street. Hawkes says its builder was Dr. Elijah Cheever, a surgeon in the Revolution, and the first of a line of scholars who made the title of Professor Cheever familiar and respected by successive classes of Harvard down to the present time.

Dr. Cheever planted his trees, laid out a private driveway and erected his house in 1806. Its exterior looks a good deal now as it did then. His brother, Col. Abner Cheever, was nearby and Col William Tudor of Rockwood not far away. Dr. Cheever was prominent in civic affairs and was often our representative in the General Court.

Celebrating 100 years as the town of Saugus

Bond collection

Cliftondale is now a section of beautiful homes and has many fruitful and beckoning themes for historical discussion, but lack of space prohibits their proper presentation in a book of this character. Its attractive village square, the enlarged Sweetser's Corner, and its many and amplified environs, very noticeably remind us of the growth of Saugus in the period covered by our present Centennial period, from just before 1815 to 1915.

Why is the most rapidly growing part of our town known as Cliftondale?

Perhaps the old Pliny Nickerson place on Essex Street, formerly the Jacob Eustis property, may suggest the answer. In 1807, about the time "Sweetser's Corner," came into prominence, this farm was owned by Jacob Eustis. He was a brother of Governor Eustis. In 1830, Jacob sold it to James Dennison, who, in turn, passed title to W. Turpin. The latter transferred it to Seth Heaton, who occupied it until 1853.

Then Daniel P. Wise and ET Ales, of Malden, appeared upon the scene, and, with them, the mystic name of "Cliftondale," by which the village name of Sweetser's Corner was relegated to the rear. The name of Cliftondale was actually suggested by Joshua Webster, first president of the Saugus Branch.

Wise and his associates began a comprehensive scheme of development, which has gone on ever since. Enterprising citizens and hustling real estate men have consistently built up the village in systematic, substantial fashion, not the booming of a busted cow-town on the western plains, but the orderly up building of a beautiful residential section near Boston and Lynn.

John T. Paine of Melrose bought a portion of the Eustis farm many years ago. Down near the Revere line, Daniel Bickford, Isaac Carleton, Charles H. Bond, Henry Waitt and Edward S. Kent were responsible for much development and building. Later, Ernest L. Nocera, in his time, built one hundred houses in Cliftondale.

The old Cliftondale Horse Railroad, of which James M. Stone of Charlestown was the manager, had a more meteoric career. It went up in 1860 and came down three years afterwards. Cars ran on it on Nov. 20, 1860. Its starting point was at the East Saugus Bridge, from which it ran on to the Cliftondale Depot, thence through the woods to the Newburyport Turnpike and so on via Malden Bridge and Charlestown.

The principal motive of its construction was to boost the sale of house lots in Cliftondale, called the 'homes,' but evidently it was not to be. Its traffic was light, which probably accounts for its brief corporate existence. Its rails were removed, and very few of the present generation perhaps can recall its existence.

The first Congregational Church – Essex Street

Bond collection

Cliftondale at rotary with tracks

Cliftondale with Bond Block on left

Cliftondale with Bond Block on left

Merchant's Row

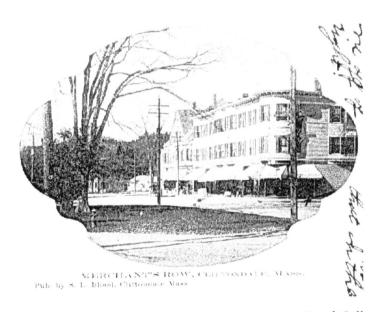

Bond Collection

Chapter II

―❧―

The Bond Family

Charles William Milton Bond
August 12, 1798 – May 1, 1884

Charles Milton Bond, Jr.
1819 – 1899

Charles Henry Bond
7-13-1846 7-3-1908

Charles Lawrence Bond
3/24/1898- 6/29/1993

Charles Dailey Bond
3-20-1932 – 11-5-2017

Note: Seven generations of Bond have borne CWMB's first name

Charles M. Bond Lot # 83, grave #12; Sally Sweetser Bond Lot #83 grave #13 both buried in Riverside Cemetery, Saugus, MA

Letter to Janice Jarosz from Charlie Bond April 11, 2006

Dear Janice: In understand that you have an interest in my grandfather, Charles H. Bond. I have some material on him and the Bonds of Cliftondale and I will get them to you tomorrow. There is more than you want I am sure but it is my guess you have a wastebasket.

I am very curious about a statement in the 1915 History of Saugus Page 75 which references the name change of the Bond/Cliftondale School. CHB died in Swampscott in July, 1908. It is possible that he had promised to build the school and that my grandmother didn't follow through with the payments. It could also reflect a reason to the possibility that he took his own life. I would love to know anything you might turn up on that subject.

Throughout his life, CHB gave 10% of his earnings to charity. In his Will he left $10,000 for the education of promising youth and the Charles H. Bond Trust gave Project Step, Inc and the Community Music School of Boston each $12,600 last year (as it does every year) for scholarship to inner city kids.

In 1968, my father gave the Cliftondale Library a large portrait size photograph of CHB who put up the original money for the library in 1884. As you can see, I enjoy the subject and, being retired, have the time to poke through the clutter of the past.

Sincerely, Charlie Bond

The following letters reflect the life and time of mid-century America.

The letters were written by members of the Amerige family and nephews of Mary Amerige Bond and first cousins of Charles Henry Bond. George and Edward Amerige founded the city of Fullerton, California, naming it for the man who made it thrive by bringing the railroad. The letters are very long but I have highlighted much of them when they discuss world events.

Lintin (China) December 7, 1832

Dear Brother:

I now take pen in hand to inform you that I have made my mind to stop off at Lintin one year longer. I was near to going home on the ship Elant, but the Captain told me if I would stop one year longer he would give me $20 a month for he could not do without me for I've been a great help to him and it's hard to get a good man that he could trust. I think it is for my interest to stop one year longer in Lintin.

You must write by the first ship bound to China and tell me how sail making, and all kinds of business is in Boston. If you think I can get plenty of work at home you must write me so and I will go home at once. I have had plenty of sail work and get well paid for it. I get four and a half dollars for working and the price in Boston is two dollars for the work. I do four different ships and my wages are 25 dollars a month but in August we had the hardest gale of wind that has been known for 20 years in China.

There were 20 sail ships laying at anchor in Capstan at the time of the gale. Some lost their masts and all of them lost more or less. The Saintin made it out without any damage. After the gale, hundreds of Chinese men, women and children were driven ashore by the waves. It is impossible to say how many Chinese boats were lost in the gale.

I am very sorry that Jonathan had that fall from his carriage. I think it must be a great setback for you. I should like to be with you to share the trouble. I hope Charles is better off than many of us and in a better place.

You must get that mad dog out of the yard before I go home. I write by a bad lamp tonight. The ships home at dawn tomorrow morning so I can't say much more tonight. I hope this will find you and all the rest of the family well. So goodbye. Your humble servant,

William Amerige.

Tell Mary that I shall think of her when I go home.

The following letter is addressed to Mrs. Mary Odiorne, to the care of Mr. Solomon Brown, Saugus Mass. (Mary's husband died probably in March and she marries CMB in November)

Amesbury, March 12, 1842

Dear Child: How can I go on with this letter when the one that took part in my former ones is gone, never to return to us but we must go to him. Let us think of his death and try to be prepared when our time comes. There is no time to prepare for death. We are too apt to think that our own days will be longer. We both have seen that in dear John. When I think of how he was taken from us, it overpowers me.

Two young men brought me to Lynn. They were very kind in regards to my feelings. They did not go by the Benning place. I will always love the dear friends of Saugus. If they had been my own, they could not have done more.

I have sent you the old stockings. I don't know if they will be of any use. You can put them in the rag bag if not. James was sick when he got the first letter. Little Emma has been sick all winter, and has had the doctor and had to have the candle.

I stayed at Hannah's upstairs in her Chamber. Sister Boardman came up they all send their love to you and feel very much for you. Sisters Offin,

Greenleaf, Grange would have come if they had known where to stop and where to go to.

Love to all, your Mother-in-law Susan G. Odiorne

A letter from Henry Amerige to Mary Amerige Bond commenting on a night of entertainment in Saugus

Boston, November 29th, 1850

Dear Sister:

It is a sense of great satisfaction to me that I am able (with a whole hand) to inform you of my safe arrival home last night. After a ride of 18 minutes I found myself safe and sound in Malden. Heartily did I laugh while on my way home at the scene I had but just passed through. Truly I am perfectly surprised at the Grand and Lofty Grumblings of a horse. The part of the performance that old Mr. Bond acted I think was done up in good shape. Take care as Charles will kick your brains out too. Don't you let him hit his head.

I took particular notice of Frank and must say that he acquitted himself in a masterly manner as the statute of Lot's wife. She never stood half so firm as Frank did. I think he could do perfect justice to Collins in the art of living statuary. And in justice to those ladies I must say that their sound was melodiously given and if Jenny Lind, the queen of songs, had been there she would have hung her head in shame.

Say to Mary Jane that I shall come down tomorrow.

Yours in Haste, Henry Amerige

San Francisco, March 31, 1853

Dear Brother and Sister – Your letter and one from Francis was received a few days ago. Keeping clear as much as I can of getting into a controversy in politics or abolition. And in favor of Pierce – hope he will not cringe to any foreign power and not make himself and not make himself by backing down on anything like Polk did on the 54 and 40 fight question.

I received a letter from Henry. He is opposed to extensions of territory. He thinks we have as much as we can attend to. I go in for making a clean sweep. John Chinaman, Japanese and Konskar – humanize them and let them go ahead in.

The politicians are about as corrupt as they can be. This state would have been well off if it had been free from the leaches that have been sucking for the last three years. They'll get such a strong hold and I'm afraid it will be hard to kick them off.

From your affectionate brother, George Amerige in a hurry.

San Francisco, Oct 20th, 1863

Dear Brother, (CMB), Sister, (AM) and little Charley (CHB) age 17

I have been writing to William. He is a good plucky little fellow. I do hope he will come out all right and that they will fight it out until they clean out the rebels and slavery and make a perfect land of liberty for the country. Arm the Negroes and let them make a clean sweep of slavery and rebellion. You affectionate Brother, G. Amerige

Camp of the 35th Regt. Mass Vol near Lyons Mills, East Tennessee, Feb 13th, 1864

Dear Aunt Mary: We are encamped five miles from Knoxville. We have nothing to do now only guard duty on picket and dress barracks every evening. The boys are all in good spirits. My regiment and the 29th Mass and 21st and 36th Mass Volunteers expect to go on an expedition which General Burnside is fitting out. We had rather go under Burnside than any other General in the Service. We have great confidence in him.

I am with my regiment now. I asked to be relieved from headquarters. My recommendation papers have gone to Governor Andrews for a commission as Lieutenant in the Colored Regt. I am very highly recommended. The officers seem to think I will get appointed and if I do, I can come home to get my uniform and will have 30 days at home. My pay then will be about $120. A month. I will have to drill the company. I think this war will not last one year. I do not see how it can. You would not think it could if you could only see the ragged, hungry, barefooted dirty looking Rebels from old Longstreet's army. Goodbye from your nephew Willie (William H. Amerige to Mary Bond, Cliftondale, Mass.)

San Francisco, June 11th, 1864

Dear Nephew: (CHB) Now that they have nominated Lincoln, I feel good. I hope he will be elected by a tremendous majority. He knows best how to manage things. Andrew Johnson will help them along with Sewage and Chase know no better man could be selected to carry the nation through and in the rebellion and restore the country and flag and clean out slavery. I say let them do it if it takes the last man and last dollar. I would like to clean out the copperheads* in our midst. They are worse than the rebels. On receipt of the news that Uncle Abe was nominated, we had a tremendous meeting. Fireworks, cannon roared, flags were flying and the whole state was rejoicing. Your affectionate Uncle George A.

*Wikipedia: In the 1860s, the Copperheads, also known as Peace Democrats, were a faction of Democrats in the Northern United States of the Union who opposed the American Civil War and wanted an immediate peace settlement with the Confederates…Republicans started calling anti-war Democrats 'copperheads' likening them to the venomous snake.

The following is a letter sent to Charles H. Bond on Saturday May 27th, 1865 from the Headquarters 2nd Division, 9th Army Corps, near Alexandria VA.

Dear Cousin Charlie:

I now take my pen in hand to write a few lines to you to let you know that I am well and I hope this letter will find you and Parents in the same health.

My regiment is to be discharged as soon as they can get our papers made out. They are to work on them now. Each company has got to have 7 muster out rolls with every man's name on them that ever belonged to the company and a full description of every man with separate discharge.

I have served two years and 10 months now. I am going right to work for Uncle Henry as soon as I get home. I shall rest about a week and go round to see the folks. I cannot bear to loaf about. I rather be at work than to be loafing. I have seen the end of the war and I have never been sorry I enlisted. I have come out of it all right and as sound as I was the day I left home. I never was so tuff as I am now…I like the service but now there is no fighting and I am anxious to get home. I do not like to play soldier. I never felt homesick – I have been through a great deal and I feel proud to think I have come out with a whole head. I remain your cousin,

William H. Amerige, Orderly.

The letter was mailed to Charles H. Bond, Cliftondale, Mass. It was canceled at Alexandria, VA, May 30 and had three cents postage due.

William was born in Saugus, Mass in 1843 and enlisted on August 1,

1862. Once discharged he went to work as a sailmaker in the Navy Shipyard, Boston, Mass.

Charles William Milton Bond

Charles William Milton Bond was born in Hampstead, New Hampshire and the son of Jonathan and Nabby (Nancy) Bond also of Hampstead, NH. For many years Mr. Bond served as a pastor of the Fourth Religious Society until he 'died suddenly' at his residence on Lime Street, May 1, 1837. A marble obelisk marks his grave in the Old Hill Burying Ground, Newburyport, MA.

The family lore is that CWMB set out to seek his fortune in the city. As he hiked along, he came to a fork in the road and had no idea which way led to Boston. As he started first down the left fork, he soon heard a bull frog rumbling, "You're wrong, you're wrong," so he returned to the fork and went right. Eventually he came to a pond full of peepers shouting, "You're right you're right." He proceeded to Saugus and the Bonds have been voting right ever since!

Sally Sweetser Bond

1795 – December 1, 1882

Bond Collection

CWMB met and eventually married Sally Sweetser of Saugus, MA. Sally was born in Saugus in 1795 to William and Lucy Sweetser. Her father, like his father and grandfather, was a manufacturer of snuff and ran a successful business in Cliftondale for many years. They had one son, Charles M. Bond, Jr., their only child, born in Saugus on August 12, 1819. Sally died in Saugus on December 1, 1882 at 87 years of age.

Note: In the 1880 census, Saugus, MA, Mr. Bond was 82 years old, living at 267-269 Lincoln Avenue; a retired cigar manufacturer and living with his wife Sally, 84, who was 'keeping house.'

Charles M. Bond, Jr, grew up in the Cliftondale area and on November 5, 1842, at the age of 23, married Miss Mary Amerige, who was also born in Saugus, Massachusetts. Mary's father, Morris Amerige, was born in 1774 in Germany; Mary was the fourth of six children.

(Note: Charles M. dropped the W from his name and listed Jr, on census records. In the 1880 Census Charles, 60, was listed as a snuff manufacturer.)

A son, Charles Henry Bond, was born at home on July 13, 1846 in the Cliftondale neighborhood of Saugus, Massachusetts. It was said that during his youth, Bond developed a love for music which would last throughout his lifetime. His grandparents lived next door.

In 1856, the Cliftondale Methodist Church was founded. At that time the entire population of the town of Saugus was fewer than 2,000 and not even 500 of that number lived in this sparsely settled section known as Cliftondale.

The church was organized on March 20, 1856 in the home of Charles Milton Bond, a two-story New England Colonial style house which occupied the site of the first post office. The building was often referred to as the 'the Methodist Headquarters.'

The first Methodist building was built on a lot of land given by Charles Sweetser, on the southerly side of Lincoln Avenue near St. Margaret's Church. Here the congregation worshipped from 1858 until a disastrous blaze of June 19, 1914 leveled the church.

However, thought had been given, prior to the fire, to the erection of a new house of worship. Negotiations had been in progress for the purchase of the Bond property at the corner of Lincoln Avenue and Jackson Street.

Charles Henry Bond

Bond collection

At age 21, Charles H. Bond became the first applicant under the Charter to apply for membership into the William Sutton Lodge of Saugus, MA. The meetings were held on October 11, 1867 and on November 14, 1867. *

From 'A Half Century of the William Sutton Lodge'

I.D. Card – Masons

Name	Bond, Charles H.		
Residence	Cliftondale	Occupation Cigar Manfgr.	Nativity Saugus 1846-7-13
Lodge	Wm. Sutton	Initiated 1868-1-2	Passed 1868-2-13	Raised 1868-3-12
Membership 1868-3-12	Dim. Sus. Dis.	Reinstated	Deceased 1908-7-3

Remarks:

Bond signature as a Mason

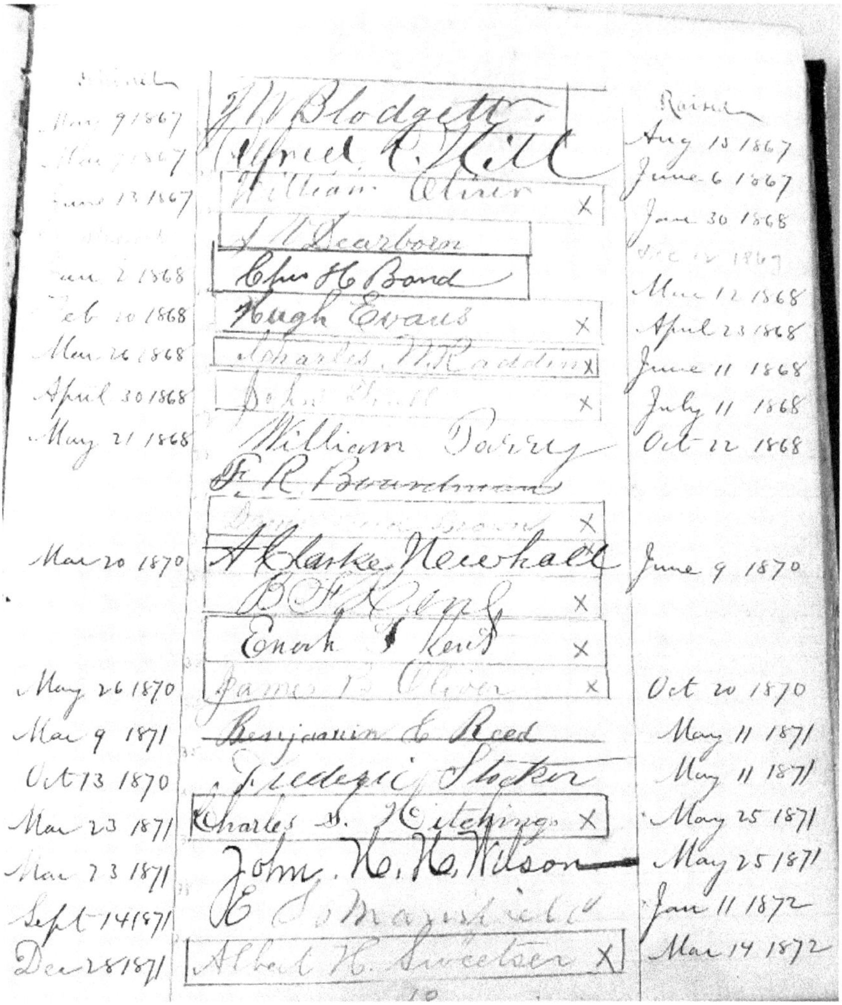

[illegible]		Raised
Mar 9 1867	J W Blodgett	Aug 13 1867
Mar [illegible] 1867	Alfred C. Hill	June 6 1867
June 13 1867	William Oliver X	June 30 1868
[illegible]	J M Dearborn	Dec 12 1867
Jan 2 1868	Chas H Bond	Mar 12 1868
Feb 20 1868	Hugh Evans X	April 23 1868
Mar 26 1868	Charles W Raddin X	June 11 1868
April 30 1868	John [illegible] X	July 11 1868
May 21 1868	William Parry	Oct 22 1868
	F R [illegible]	
	[illegible] Brown X	
Mar 20 1870	A Clarke Newhall	June 9 1870
	B F [illegible] X	
	Enoch [illegible] Kent X	
May 26 1870	James B Oliver X	Oct 20 1870
Mar 9 1871	Benjamin E Reed	May 11 1871
Oct 13 1870	Frederic Stocker	May 11 1871
Mar 23 1871	Charles H. Hitchings X	May 25 1871
Mar 23 1871	John H. H. Wilson	May 25 1871
Sept 14 1871	E S [illegible]	Jan 11 1872
Dec 28 1871	Albert H. Sweetser X	Mar 14 1872

Personal Sketch

PERSONAL SKETCH.

Charles Henry Bond

Chas. H. Bond was born in Sangus July 3rd 1843 the only child of Charles Melton Bond and Mary Ambrose Bond.

He graduated from Stone and Sawyer's Commercial College in Boston and started business for himself at the age of seventeen, later became the founder of the Waitt and Bond Blackstone Cigar Co.

He first married Miss Martha A. Morrison of Lawrence, who died in 1881, leaving two children Sara and Charlie H.

His second wife was Miss Isabella Bacon of Washington, D.C. by whom he had six children, Edith, Mildred, Kenneth, Charles Lawrence, and Priscilla.

Mr. Bond was a great lover of art, the drama and music, and he did a great deal to aid young students in completing their musical and professional education. In 1885 he gave to his native village books for a Public library.

He was one of the original members of the Saugus Water Board and was President of the Musical Welfare Club. He was also on the Standing Committee of the Second Unitarian Church of Boston for years. He belonged to the Boston Art Club and was a member of the Sons of Colonial Wars. He was a Knight Templar Mason.

For a number of years he furnished the Bond Prizes for the graduating classes for the best essays at the High School in Saugus. To the local Camp of Sons of Veterans Mr. Bond presented their Lady Arms and Colors on Feb 8th 1894. The Camp was named for him.

Mr. Bond also furnished entertainments at the Soldiers Home in Chelsea for the Gen. C. W. Kinsley Post #139 G.A.R. July 25th 1883, Nov. 27th 1885, May 25th 1886, July 11th 1887.

He also gave a Musical and Literary entertainment at Town Hall Saugus, Monday evening April 21st 1902 under the auspices of Gen. C. W. Kinsley Post #139 G.A.R.

Mr. Bond was a genial companion, a staunch friend and a benefactor to all in need.

Bond Prize Recitations Program Cover

Bond collection

Two-page letter from George Bacon

Bond Collection

THE BOND FAMILY 61

Letter with envelope attached

Bond Collection

Odd Fellows Hall, Jackson Street

I. O. O. F. Hall.

Bond collection

In the early 1880's, Mr. Bond purchased the Odd Fellows Building, formerly an empty tobacco factory, and proceeded to refurbish it. The second floor, named Clifton Hall, was used for entertainment for the townsfolk. Bond hired and paid musicians, orchestras, lectureres, and actors for entertainment. These events were so pleasing to the patrons that a Union Society was formed to keep the entertainment going.

Mr. Bond gave the admission charges equally to all of the churches of Saugus, regardless of their denomination.

A Letter to Miss Bacon

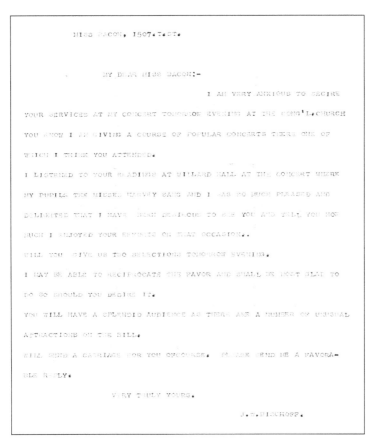

Bond collection

The early years of Charles Henry Bond

Growing up in Cliftondale, Charles attended local schools and, upon graduation, followed in the footsteps of his father and grandfather, who were in the tobacco industry, by selling cigars purchased from Henry Waitt of Franklin Park, North Revere.

He soon learned that he needed to know something about accounting, so he attended Spencer College of Business in Boston. Mr. Waitt was so impressed with the increased sales developed by Mr. Bond, that he suggested they form a partnership in 1867 and thus was started the firm Waitt and Bond. Mr. Waite made cheroots in his Franklin Park, Revere home and CHB sold them. Later, when they needed more space and a larger labor force, they moved to Boston, locating on Blackstone Street, and their product was named Blackstone Cigars.

The Bond Mansion

Bond Collection

Charles Bond Charter – 1846

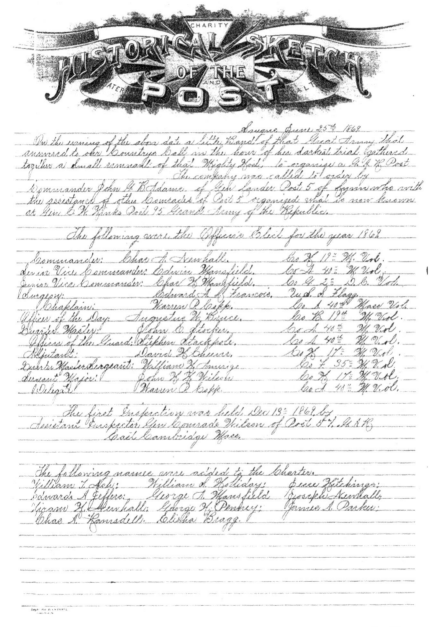

Bond collection

As early as 1873, real estate development became a major interest for Charles. After a successful project in Malden, he undertook the development of land in Cliftondale. With two other Saugus businessmen, they purchased and developed the area westerly of Lincoln Avenue from North Revere and southerly off Cliftondale Square. With a fortune accumulated from his cigar business, Bond became involved in real estate and became one of the largest holders of real estate in Boston.

Eventually Charles moved up Lincoln Avenue into his grandfather's home at the corner of Lincoln Ave. and Jackson St. He married Martha Augusta, daughter of Benjamin P. Morris and Sarah (Wentworth) Morris, and was born in Buxton, Maine, in 1872. Unfortunately, Martha died in 1881 from childbed fever leaving two children Sara and Charles Wadsworth. Son Charles W. passed away on September 10, 1881.

After the death of his wife and son, he devoted much of his time in helping young people get started in musical careers or the theater. Throughout his life he demonstrated his belief in the importance of education by providing financial assistance to young people. One, Geraldine Farrar of Melrose, was to become a world-renowned opera singer - another, Alina Barentzen of Somerville, a renowned pianist and professor at the Paris Conservatory, Melrose, MA.

Isabella Bacon Bond
1859-01-02-1931

Bond collection

Charles takes a second wife

On May 1, 1883, at the age of 36, Charles married Isabella Bacon, 23, in Saugus, Massachusetts. Isabella was raised in Boston, Mass, Melrose, Mass and 1057 T St, NW, Washington, D.C. She attended the Winthrop School of Boston, the present site of the Wilbur Theater and graduated from Melrose High School in 1878.

(From a portrait painted by Emily Burlingame Waite)

Obituary of George Bacon

WAS AN ACTIVE WORKER IN ANTI-SLAVERY CAUSE.

George A. Bacon, Whose Death Is Announced, Was Associated with Phillips and Garrison.

George A. Bacon, whose death was announced yesterday, was born at Wellfleet in 1830. He came to Boston when 10 years of age, with his parents, and resided here until the civil war. Of literary tastes he continually used his pen for the advancement of every movement which tended toward higher and broader civilization. He was an active worker in the anti-slavery movement, being associated with Phillips and Garrison, and a strong believer in woman suffrage.

He was an ardent Baconian, and published much regarding the Bacon-Shakespeare controversy. In later years as a student of comparative religions he wrote and published a clear, comprehensive and concise pamphlet upon Buddha and his teachings.

He entered the war department in Washington in 1861, later the agricultural department, from which he was afterward transferred to the civil service commission, which position he retained until his resignation, on account of health, last April.

His widow was formerly Miss Louise Lynde of Melrose, and his daughter, Mrs. Charles H. Bond of Boston, is well known in musical, patriotic and philanthropic circles. For the past two months he resided at his daughter's former home in Cliftondale.

Thank you note from George Amerige January 7, 1885

> Cliftondale, Jan. 7, 1885.
>
> Charles H. Bond, Esq.
> My dear Sir:
>
> At a meeting of the Citizens of Cliftondale, held Dec. 29th, 1884, for the purpose of taking action concerning the acceptance of your very generous offer of the sum of Five Hundred Dollars to found a Public Library in our village, a Committee consisting of Mr. M. V. Putnam, Mr. W. W. Martin, Mr. A. B. Coates, Miss A. R. Putnam and the undersigned, was chosen to confer with you and ascertain your views and wishes in relation to the Library and Association, and the proper methods of conducting the same.
>
> The Committee will be pleased to wait upon you for the purpose indicated, at your convenience.
>
> Very truly Yours
> George M. Amerige
> for the Committee

Bond collection

Robert Ingersoll – a man in love with the golden leaf

Bond collection

Mr. Charles H. Bond:

My dear friend: I received the cigar. It is the largest tobacco saw log, the longest clear Havana liberty pole that I ever saw. On the thirteenth day of next February, I shall smoke the cigar-that is my wedding day-and I will think of you between puffs.

I shall wish you and yours the happiest of all lives and that all your troubles may end in smoke. Accept my thanks for your most appropriate present. Were it not for tobacco the world would be a dull and dreary place?

I am proud of the fact that America gave that precious plant to the human race. It is a perpetual joy and a continual consolation. It fills homes with a "peace that passeth human understanding." For it enables us to bear the ills we have and to care nothing for we know not of. It makes us social, sympathetic, polite, good-natured, and even virtuous. It belongs to the fireside and makes home a kind of paradise.

Thanking you again for that cigar and wishing you and your wife joys equal to those that tobacco can give, I remain,

        Yours always,

               Robert Ingersoll

'Smoke Blackstone Cigars'

Bond collection

Bill to Charles H. Bond from Waitt 1874

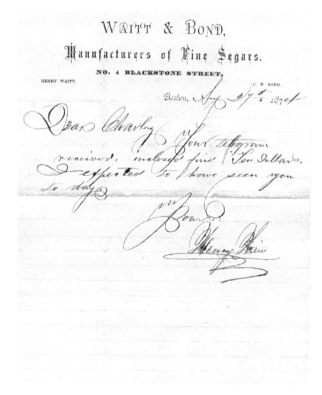

Bond collection

Note: John William Bischoff became blind at the age of two but went on to become one of the most famous organists in the country. He composed many songs including God be with You, and Not half Has Been Told, to name a few. He served as the principal organist at the first Congregational Church in Washington from 1874 until his passing in 1909. Interestingly, he divorced his first wife and married Elise Bond.

Letter from Belle to Mama 1887

```
                                    CLIFTONDALE, JULY 2, 1887.
MY DEAR MAMMA,-
              YOUR SUNDAY LETTER WAS AWAITING ME AT
THE BREAKFAST-TABLE THIS MORNING, IN COMPANY WITH ONE
FROM ANNIE CURRIER, WHOM I HAVE NOT HEARD FROM for
NEARLY TWO YEARS I SHOULD SAY.
                         LAST EVE I READ AT THE
SOLDIERS HOME. MISS DREW & MISS NICHOLS SANG.   IT
WAS SO DULL THAT THE  BARGES DID NOT GO OVER FROM HERE.
              IT RAINED A GOOD PART OF YESTER-
-DAY, FOR WHICH I AM VERY THANKFUL AS WE NEED IT VERY
MUCH.
        I HOPE YOU WILL GET HERE BY FRIDAY. ON THURS-
DAY WE HAVE OUR SUNDAY-SCHOOL PICNIC, AND I SUPPOSE WE
SHALL ALL HAVE TO GO.
              TODAY I AM TO MEET THE SELECT-
-MEN AND INSPECT OUR SCHOOL BUILDINGS TO SEE WHAT NEW
IMPROVMENTS CAN BE MADE.  I HAVE PLENTY OF THINGS THAT
I WANT THEM TO DO IF THEY CAN AFFORD IT
                                   MY SEWING IS
NEARLY DONE I THINK, LIZZIE WILL FINISH THIS WEEK &
LEAVE FOR THE SUMMER.
              I HOPE PAPA WILL MAKE MORE RAPID
ADVANCEMENT IN MANIPULATING HIS TYPE-WRITER THAN I DO
WITH MINE. PLEASE TELL HIM THAT MINE IS CALLED THE
WORLD TYPE WRITER. IT IS A SMALL INSTRUMENT THAT I CAN
HOLD IN MY LAP IF I WANT TO.
              GRACE WAS OVER AND STAID OVER
NIGHT WITH SADIE LAST WEEK.   FRANK IS THINKING OF GOING
TO FITCHBURG TO WORK IN A MACHINE SHOP
                              AUSTIN SAW WILLIAM
O'CONNOR IN CALIFORNIA  HE TOLD MARIA THAT W-  LOOKED
A PERFECT WRECK.
              NOW I MUST GO TO WORK.
     LOVE TO PAPA & YOURSELF
                              AFF.
                                   BELLE.
```

Bond collection

From the Memoires of Isabella Bacon Bond

Cliftondale, in 1883, was a lovely rural village with one principal street winding between the city of Lynn on the east and Malden on the southwest. It had one schoolhouse, one church, a general store and post office.

My new home was a large, square, finely-proportioned house built by the famous Norcross Brothers. It was erected in the 1870's for George Sweetser, who was State Senator and a cousin of Charlie's who died soon after its completion. As Mr. Sweetser's family was not able to maintain so large and expensive an establishment, Charlie bought it. The house was well located at the corner of Jackson Street and Lincoln Avenue where that thoroughfare suddenly took an almost right-angle south.

On the same lot originally had stood the old Houghton Homestead, which years before had been moved down the avenue a short distance and put back from the street. At the time the Sweetser mansion was erected, Charlie and his family were living in the house he had built when he married Augusta Morrison of Lawrence, Massachusetts, in 1872, which adjoined the Sweetser place. In 1881, while in the process of decorating and furnishing the new home Augusta was taken ill and passed away in a few days. Charlie at once countermanded all orders and lost interest for the time in completing the work.

After we were married, he gave me cart-blanche to have the furnishings completed according to my own taste. Then, my first responsibility in home-making proved a real pleasure and a valuable experience.

On the same side of the avenue, three houses east of ours stood the home of Charlie's paternal grandfather, built about 1685. The bricks had been brought from England. Grandfather Charles W. Milton Bond, who married Sally Sweetser in 1818, had gone to live in this old house with his bride. It was she who had died less than a month after my grandfather Bacon's death in 1882.

Charlie's grandfather came to call on me soon after my arrival in Cliftondale. He was one of the tallest men I have ever seen, and although then 85, was so erect that he almost bent backwards. I remember his first words to me; "Belle, I am very deaf and cannot hear a word you say. But I will ask you questions that can be answered by 'yes' or 'no.' So you may bob your head and then I will understand." I found him so clever in formulating his questions that it was interesting to study his method.

The following spring, on May 12, 1884, after a few days of indisposition, he sent for us to come to him. As I knelt beside his sofa, he took my hand and said he knew me, and then taking my face between his hands, called me by name and said, "My dear grand-daughter I want to meet you on the other side." He said he was quite resigned to go. We left him soon after and at midnight he passed quietly away.

It had been in the parlor of his house, not long after he was married, that the Methodist Episcopal Society was organized. Services were held there until the Society could afford to erect a church. The house remained standing until 1900, when it was taken down as not being safe for occupancy.

The next house to Grandfather's on the east was a white one in which Charlie's father still lived. It was there that Charlie was born in 1846. Charlie, like myself, was an only child. He and his mother were devoted to each other. When he was sixteen, she became an invalid and was confined to her bed for eleven years before she died. Never during all those years did he ever hear her complain of her condition in spite of great suffering. And never did he fail on returning from school, or from business, to go to her room at once. He has told me that before her illness she was full of life and fun, with a desire to make people happy.

Bond Collection

The Charles Henry Bond family lived in Cliftondale from 1883 to 1890 and were the parents of five children, Edith, Kenneth B, Charles D, Lawrence and Pricilla I. Pricilla died at age 4 on April 26, 1904 after suffering for 10 days with diphtheria. She was removed to the Mass Crematory.

While becoming increasingly busy with the tobacco business and raising a family, Mr. Bond still found time to set up the first Saugus public library in his home in 1885, and later served as chairman of the Board of Trustees for the Library. He also served on the first Water Board for the town of Saugus, and financially organized and supported the Charles H. Bond Sons of the Union Veterans Camp 104s condominiums.

128 Commonwealth Avenue, Boston, MA

Front Foyer

Bond Collection

The family moved to 128 Commonwealth Avenue in Boston in 1893. There Mr. Charles H. Bond employed one servant, one cook, two nurses and one butler.

Bond was a staunch member of the Republican Party. He was occasionally involved in politics, but never held elected office. He was also a member of numerous clubs and fraternal organizations, including the Freemasons, Knights Templar, the Tedesco Country Club, and the Sons of Colonial Wars.

In the 1890's, real estate development became his major interest and he undertook land development projects in Cliftondale and Malden as well as commercial properties in Boston, MA and Washington D.C.

Front of Washington D.C. building

Bond collection

Bond finally gets his name on a building

Bond Collection

The Bond Building, completed in 1901 for an estimated $300,000, was designed by George S. Cooper, who had learned his trade in part as an apprentice in the prestigious Washington firms of Hornblower & Marshall.

Cooper reflected his Beaux-Arts training in the elaborate classical ornamentation where he chose to articulate the five ascending stages of the building's imposing façade. The arches rise from a white marble first floor through a soaring arcade in the third through fifth floor, and are crowned by a massive swaged entablature, heavy dentilated cornice, and surmounting balustrade.

Our early 21st-century eyes, weary of the plainness of contemporary buildings, tend to be quite taken by this riot of Gilded-Age decoration. However, because it's simply ornamental, it is difficult to make a case for it being great architecture.

In fact, former *Washington Post* critic Benjamin Forgey called it a "rather hectic wedding cake of classic revival motifs," although he nonetheless deemed it a 'treasure.' "The Bond has a lot of personality sort of highfalutin street-wise charm. Indeed."

With 'Bond Building' prominently inscribed on both sides of its facade, the structure's principal investor is difficult to ignore. Bond was apparently not by any means your typical, ruthless Gilded-Age industrialist. In fact, he apparently had little interest in the cigar business once he had made his fortune. His real love had always been for music and the performing arts. He took his support of aspiring young singers as his personal mission.

Quoting again from the 1909 Biographical History of Massachusetts, Bond "had ever a listening ear and an open hand for young men and women struggling for an education." He gave prizes to promising students in a number of schools, including prizes specifically for African-American students at New Orleans University.

An article written for *The Washington Post* at the time of Bond's death gives more specifics: "Through his aid several young women attained fame as singers, for whenever a voice interested him and the owner could not afford to cultivate it, he paid her expenses for training in this country and abroad. Among these were Geraldine Farrar, May Pendergast, and Ada Chambers, of New York. He allowed them $100 a month for their living expenses which gave them a thorough training by the best European masters."

Charles continued to support worthy causes. He loaned money to start a local YMCA and loaned his home to them for headquarters. He worked hard for causes that benefited his hometown and gave generously to the churches.

The tobacco business grew rapidly and in 1890's, Waitt and Bond built a factory at Stillman and Endicott's Streets, Boston, MA. Expanding further a few years later they set up a second factory at 4 Blackstone Street, Boston, MA and 'Blackstone' became the name of their most popular cigar. It wasn't long before Waitt and Bond grew to become one of the largest cigar manufacturers in New England and one of the largest in the United States at the time.

It was well-known that cigars were often made in buildings of considerable size such as Waitt and Bond in Boston who employed 648 workers in 1913. At Waitt and Bond, where male workers were unionized, opening hours there was no constraint on the performance of workers except that they produce good quality, and that they maintain on average a reasonable output. Workers came and left when the wanted, socialized at work and set their own output levels.

Bond home burns to the ground - lit candle suspected

Bond collection

Charles kept strong ties in Cliftondale throughout his lifetime. His first home remained in the Bond family as his daughter married Frederick H. Stearns and the newlyweds moved into the home.

In the winter of 1915, smoke was discovered, and the house was destroyed by fire. Some believed it was from a candle. Mr. Stearns, a noted artist, lost over 100 paintings. The property was eventually given to the Methodist Church in Cliftondale whose original building had burned to the ground in 1914 and a new Methodist church was built in 1916 on the site of the Bond Mansion property.

Insurance Letter

A. H. SAWYER, PRESIDENT.   Established 1853   W. H. STEVENS, SEC'T AND TREAS.

PERSONAL.   WATERTOWN, N. Y., Dec. 24, 1900.

Charles H. Bond, Esq.,
    C/o Waitt & Bond,
        No. 53 Blackstone St., Boston, Mass.

Dear Sir:-

    Our Boston Manager has just informed us of the circumstances relative to the discovery of additional insurance in the "Spring Garden" insurance company, on your property which was destroyed by fire in September, 1899, on which we paid the total amount of the loss.

    Permit us to say that it is indeed refreshing and encouraging to find a policy-holder who does not regard insurance companies as more or less thieves and robbers and fit subjects for deception. The companies, as a rule, have to bear their full proportion of odium and rarely receive their due share of consideration and approbation.

        Yours very truly,

                Sec'y.

Letter from Franklin Square Home

The Franklin Square House.
George L. Perin, President
Albert Metcalf, Treasurer

Telephone No. 252 Tremont

Boston, May 17, 1902, 190

Mr. Charles H. Bond,
   53 Blackstone St.,
      Boston, Mass.

Dear Mr. Bond:-

      I have just received yours enclosing check for $1000 to be used in establishing the Franklin Square House for working girls. I want to thank you sincerely for this expression of your interest in this work. I hope that we shall justify your confidence and your generosity in the good that we shall do.

      I was exceedingly sorry to hear of the death of Mr. Waite. It must impose upon you heavier responsibility.

      Thanking you again for your kindness, I am

          Yours sincerely,

          George L. Perin

Bond collection

Mr. Bond donated Saugus land to the Congregational Church and another lot for a church parsonage. His donations to the Saugus camp of the Sons of Union Veterans of the Civil War were credited for its success; the camp was named in Bond's honor. Mr. Bond also furnished entertainment at the Soldiers Home in Chelsea for the General E.W. Hinks Post #95 on many occasions.

The many gifts Charles H. Bond

On Sundays Mr. Bond hired student ministers to conduct religious services. A Sunday school was established and in early 1888, student minister Andrew Archibald conducted church services for about 50 people. A Congregationalist, Mr. Archibald was approached by some of the people about forming a church. Adhering to the laws of the Commonwealth of Massachusetts and the Congregational Church, the church opened its doors on May 7, 1888 as the First Congregational Society of Cliftondale.

This Church burned to the ground in 1914, and on June 19, 1915, the property, originally the site of the Bond Mansion, was acquired by the Cliftondale Methodist Church.

With $700.00 in the building fund, it was voted to apply to the Congregational Church Building Society for aid. A gift of $500.00 and a loan of $1,000.00 was granted on October 23, 1891. Mr. Bond, the owner of the land, sold it to the church for $1.00 and construction was started immediately.

A patron of the arts, he provided funding for the training of many vocal artists. He was a member of the Boston Arts Club and served on its entertainment committee. Bond was also a trustee of the New England Conservatory of Music.

Throughout his life, CHB committed 10% of his income to charitable works. Instead of giving cash to a music student, he rented a theater and provided the advertising so the gate could go to the student. He also provided financial support to the New England Conservatory, Emerson College, the Leland Powers School, the North Bennett Street Industrial School and the Franklin Square House.

Bond offered an award known as the Bond Speaking Prize to the most proficient students at Saugus High School, Wesleyan University, and New Orleans University. He also aided students at St. Lawrence University.

A Unitarian, Bond was a member of the Second Church of Boston. For many years he was a member of the church's standing committee as well as its music committee. During his later years, Bond became interested in Christian Science.

The Bonds Summer at 'Peace Haven' Swampscott, Mass

Bond collection

Mr. Bond bought a large summer home on Paradise (Puritan) Road in Swampscott for his family, and to quote him, "to enjoy the ocean and the ocean breezes."

Front door

Bedroom

Sitting Room

Isabella Bacon Bond in her Peace Haven Garden

Bond collection

A note from a Bond family member

There were three summer hotels in Swampscott; the Lincoln House, at the west end of the beach; the Ocean House, diagonally across Puritan Road from our house; and the Little Anawan which was more like a boarding house at the east end of the beach. Papa was friendly with Mr. Grabau, the manager of the Ocean House and used to supply him with protégé artistes for Sunday evening entertainment. Thus, he helped the performers, whom he paid, and the guests with a free concert.

For many years, Charles H. Bond was an associate member of Sons of Union Veterans of the Civil War, Post 104, and a member of the William Sutton Lodge, Scottish Rite Masons of Saugus.

Nat Bond, a grandson, shared a story with me in 2007

'Shortly before his death, CHB realized that his cigar factory had to grow, and he began to plan a new facility off of Columbus Avenue on Burke Street in South Boston, or the South End… I never knew the difference. The building, designed by Densmore and LeClair, opened in 1912. Eventually Waitt and Bond was purchased by JA Cigars and relocated to New Jersey. The building was sold and I knew nothing of its history until it was purchased in the 1990's by Northeastern University. It is now an office building for faculty and administrators.'

Charles H. Bond died 3 July 1908 at 61 years of age while at his summer home in Swampscott, MA. Funeral services were held from his late residence, "Peace Haven" Swampscott, MA. at 1:00 o'clock; the service being of a strictly private nature, only the immediate relatives of the family being in attendance. The family had requested no flowers, but there were a number of beautiful floral tributes from very dear business and social friends.

The services were those of the Christian Science faith and Rev. William P. McKenzie, a Christian Science practitioner of Cambridge, presided. Miss Eva Dine, a protégé of Boston and a student at the New England Conservatory, sang "Abide by Me," it being one of Mr. Bond's favorite hymns. After the services, the remains were conveyed over the road to Mt. Auburn Cemetery, Forest Hills, were his body was cremated.

After his death a concert was given in Boston by artists that he had assisted.

Editor's note: The death of Mr. Bond was ruled accidental

The Boston Traveler wrote about Charles H. Bond

"The Will of the late Charles H. Bond emphasizes the public-spirited characteristics of the man. In an unostentatious way, Mr. Bond gave freely during his life to deserving young people of ability for the advancement of musical and industrial education, giving them the best musical instruction possible in this country and abroad."

In his will he left $10,000.00 for the education of promising youth. The Charles H. Bond Trust gave Project Step, Inc., and the Community Music Center of Boston which annually grants over $25,000.00 each year for scholarships for inner city kids. He provided Saugus High School and other schools with awards for academic achievement.

During his lifetime he helped found the Sons of Union Veterans of the Civil War and donated its colors and side arms and endowed the post with an annual income. In 1957 his estate made a grant to the Charles H Bond Post 104 Post replacing the annual stipend. It now meets in Wakefield, MA.

A Unitarian, Bond was a member of the Second Church of Boston. For many years he was a member of the church's standing committee as well as its music committee.

After his death and for many years thereafter until her passing in 1931, Isabella Bacon Bond carried on CHB's charitable work in music and theater. She donated money for Bond Hall to be built in his honor at the MacDowell Colony in Peterborough, New Hampshire. She also traveled to Europe on many occasions.

Philanthropist Charles H. Bond Found Dead at Summer Residence

Wife found body lying face down in several inches of water in bath tub at early hour Friday night

Incomplete note in deceased's handwriting found in bedroom.

Profound regret among community over strange and untimely passing of benefactor of worthy young men and women

Laying face downward, in a bath tub filled with water, the body of Charles Henry Bond, one of Boston's philanthropic citizens, was discovered by a Japanese servant in the private apartment of his employer at the latter's palatial summer home at 233 Puritan Road, Swampscott, early Friday evening, under circumstances which appeared to indicate that death resulted from a deliberate and premeditated attempt at self-destruction.

Inasmuch as Medical Examiner Pinkham, who viewed the body more than four hours after dissolution occurred, was not officially required to designate whether death had resulted from an accident or from a suicidal attempt, the certificate signed Saturday noon showed that drowning was a cause of death.

Charles Henry Bond, President and General Manager of Waitt & Bond, Inc., New England's largest cigar manufacturing firm, was a native of Cliftondale, and from the time he began the manufacture of cigars, 44 years ago, in a little shop on Lincoln Avenue, Saugus, fortune smiled upon him and the business increased to such an extent that Mr. Bond became known as one of Boston's multi-millionaires.

A patron of art and music, and a man identified with Boston's best known institutions devoted to the instruction of music, he was particularly well known in musical circles, and his extensive real estate holdings in Boston, Washington D.C. and along the North Shore, brought to him a reputation which extended over the eastern section of the country.

His sudden death, announcement of which was withheld for almost 12 hours subsequent to its occurrence, was not received with expressions of great surprise among business men with whom he had held intimate relations, but sentiments of regret, all bearing the ring of true sincerity, were forthcoming when news of his demise had been disseminated.

According to information given to newspaper men by a representative of the Bond family, Mr. Bond returned from his office in Boston early Friday afternoon, and as had been his custom, he immediately retired to his private apartment for an afternoon siesta. When he failed to appear for dinner at 6 o'clock, Mrs. Bond became worried and an hour later the Japanese butler was sent to Mr. Bond's room to call him. Finding the door affording entrance to the apartment securely locked, the servant succeeded in gaining entrance to the room by climbing through a window and going to the bathroom and found the body of Mr. Bond in the bath tub.

In the bedroom adjoining, lying upon a table a note was found, written on the back of an envelope, as if hurriedly, bearing no signature, but in the handwriting of Mr. Bond. It was short and apparently in an incomplete condition. This was substantially worded: "Killed by my friends and enemies, my heart is broken. I leave everything to Bella."

The note was carefully preserved by a daughter of the deceased, was not made public, but among other things which Mr. Bond wrote, in a peculiarly unusual manner, was the fact that his heart was weak and that he had many friends and some enemies. There appeared to be no consistency to the sentence in which the words, 'friends and enemies' appeared and the following sentence, which was construed to be related to his estate, was, according to the Item's informant, fragmentary, and of no particular importance. There was no mention whatever made by the writer that his financial condition had caused him to seek death.

Following the summoning of Mrs. Bond, after the body had been found, Dr. Harry C. Low, of Puritan Road, was called but death had occurred at least two hours before his arrival. The physician, later in the evening, consulted with Dr. Loring Grimes, of the Swampscott Board of Health in regard to the case. Dr. Low, following the termination of the interview with town officials, thereupon notified Medical Examiner Pinkham who immediately visited the Bond residence, one of the most expensive summer homes along the North Shore.

Dr. Pinkham remained in the house for a long period of time, but although an offer to show him the note found in the bedroom was made, just prior to his departure, he did not see the paper as he expressed no desire to do so.

In conversation with an Item reporter Saturday, Dr. Pinkham stated that he had signed the certificate subscribing drowning as the cause of death, but no other information would be given out by the Medical

Examiner. Every effort was made to conceal from the newspaper man the fact that Mr. Bond was found dead in the bath tub but Saturday forenoon it was asserted that he had been stricken with heart failure and had dropped dead in his dressing room just after he had taken a cold bath.

Charles Henry Bond was born in Cliftondale, July 13, 1846, and was the son of Charles M. and Mary Amerige Bond. He received his early education in the town schools and then attended two business schools in Boston. At the age of 17, when he had a capital of $17.00, he formed a partnership with Henry Waitt, also of Saugus, and began the manufacture of cigars in the little Lincoln Avenue shop. The business flourished and step and step the branch moved on until it became necessary to seek larger quarters, and the big plan of Waitt & Bond at 67 Endicott Street, Boston, was acquired.

Besides attending to the management of the extensive cigar business, Mr. Bond had been interested in various other successful enterprises, and according to his intimate friends, the strain became too great several months ago and his nerves became unstrung. He sought relief from a Christian Science healer, for he was a member of that cult, but his efforts to fight off the trouble were not successful.

On May 15, the Charles H. Bond Corporation was organized with a capital of $1,000,000, with Mr. Bond as President. It was chartered under Massachusetts laws for 'the building and construction, the managing of hotels, etc.' John C.F. Slayton and Arthur W. Newell of Lexington and all of the extensive properties which he had purchased were turned over to those two men, who have since been managing the business as far as real estate transactions were concerned. It was publicly stated at the time of the transfer of the properties that the purpose was 'to relieve Mr. Bond of the care incident to the handling of his extensive real estate investments.'

Mr. Bond's real estate ventures amassed Boston bankers and the purchases which he made gave rise to the opinion that his fortune was not great enough to swing the project. Neither Mr. Slayton nor Mr. Newell would discuss Mr. Bond's financial condition Saturday other than to say that he was perfectly solvent.

Last December, Mr. Bond bought Brandon Hall, in Brookline, for about $225,000. In April he purchased the estate at 482-546 Boylston Street assessed at $194,000. Then he bought the Hotel Netherland, on Boylston Street, and the building is not being renovated. He also acquired possession of the Oceanside at Magnolia, and obtained a long lease with the Hotel Baltic, in Boston.

He tried to buy the A. Shuman Corner, at Boylston and Washington Streets, and it was stated that he was desirous of acquiring the adjoining property and that he eventually intended to have an immense hotel on the entire site. The Webster estate, opposite the Massachusetts Institute of Technology, on Boylston Street, was another of his purchases.

In April, he made the announcement that he would build a half million dollar theater on Tremont Street, to be known as the Lyric, but just what effect his death will have upon the carrying out of his plans cannot be foretold. It was reckoned by Boston real estate men that Mr. Bond's purchases cost him almost $2,000,000.00.

In another light of Mr. Bond, was his benevolence. Many young women and men have gained fame in the opera world, and but for him, they could not have received the training which prepared them for musical circles. Geraldine Farrar, of Melrose, now world famous as a prima donna, was assisted by him, and two talented young New York women, Miss May Prendergast and Miss Ada Chambers, owe their success to him. He was a subscriber to the Symphony Concerts, the Cecilia and Handel and Hayden and other musical societies of Boston.

His home life was particularity pleasant. His first wife was Martha Morrison of Lawrence, and their only child is Mrs. S. Pomerory Todd, of Los Angeles, Cal. His second wife, who survives, is Bella Bacon, who was prominent in Washington society before her marriage. She was a reader and was active in amateur theatricals. Since her marriage she has entertained extensively and has assisted her husband in developing the talents of deserving young persons.

The Bond home in Swampscott, 'Peace Haven' has been noted for the splendor of the entertainments given there, and every season several concerts have been given at which artists who had Mr. Bond's patronage repaid him somewhat for his philanthropy.

Up to 1899, Mr. Bond resided in a beautiful home in Cliftondale, and he has ever been ready to assist the public projects in that part of Saugus. He was one of the original members of the Saugus Water Board, was President of the Cliftondale Library Association, to whom he gave books, Trustee of the Saugus Library, and he had been of great financial assistance to Charles H. Bond Camp, Sons of Veterans, of Saugus. His winter home was at Commonwealth Avenue, Boston and there his entertainments were among the most extensive given in the city.

Funeral services were held from his late residence, 'Peace Haven' Puritan Road, Swampscott at 1:00 'clock this afternoon, the service being of a strictly private nature, only the immediate relatives of the family being in attendance. The family had requested no flowers, but there were a number of beautiful tributes from very dear business and social friends. During the morning hours, a large number of summer residents called to express condolences and a number of telegrams and cablegrams were received containing messages of sympathy.

The services were those of the Christian Science faith, of which the deceased was an interested worker with Rev. William P. McKenzie, a

Christian Science practitioner of Cambridge, and a former pastor of the Cambridge Congregational Church. Miss Eva Dine, of Boston, a protégé and a student at the New England Conservatory of Music, sang in a beautiful voice, 'Abide with Me,' it being one of the deceased favorite hymn. After the services, the remains were conveyed over the road to Mt. Auburn Cemetery, Forest Hills, where the body will be cremated.

By the death of Charles H. Bond, after executing an indenture of trust to John F. C. Slayton and Arthur N. Newell, the State will not get the revenue from the inheritance tax or the collateral legacy tax, which it would have obtained had he died testate and bequeathed his property by Will. Under the provisions of the statute, such action upon the part of a testator, in disposing of his property before death, exempts the executors or administrators from payment of such tax. The fact that, by the deed of trust, the trustees named are empowered to issue 1,000 shares of common and not exceeding 10,000 shares of preferred stock, the latter at a par value of $1,000, with six percent, cumulative dividends, indicates that the deceased was many times a millionaire. In his conveyance to the trustees, the late Mr. Bond named no less than 12 valuable parcels of real estate in Boston, some of which is heavily mortgaged, but much more if it is not.

It includes Haddon Hall, on the corner of Clarendon Street and Commonwealth Avenue, the Hotel Netherlands, the former Lexington Hotel and other properties. Had it not been for the indenture of trust, the Treasury of the Commonwealth would have received a very considerable sum by way of the inheritance tax. The estate of the late Quincy A. Shaw of Boston may escape the same way.

(Article from the Lynn Item Newspaper, July 3, 1908)

The Settling of the Bond Estate

Taken from the Lynn Item, July 7, 1908

Trustees Will Make No Statement Concerning Their Plans for the Future
Some Properties Will be Kept
Statements of the Wife and Daughter Touching Upon Suicide Theory

Boston financial circles are evidencing an unusual interest in the settlement of the affairs of Charles Henry Bond, who was found dead in his bath tub, at his Swampscott summer residence last Friday night. It was expected that C.F. Slayton and Arthur W. Newell, Trustees of the estate, and other intimate business associates, who met this noon at 19 Blackstone Street, Boston, would discuss matters in connection with the trust and would determine what policies would be pursued relative to the carrying out or dropping the extensive plans which Mr. Bond had prepared for the development of his immense real estate holdings.

It appeared to be the general opinion among Boston real estate men, Monday, that the Trustees would decide to dispose of Mr. Bond's theatrical and hotel enterprises as quickly as the opportunities are available. Neither of the Trustees would consent to talk for publication in regard to their opinion as to the wisest course to follow in settling the Bond estate affairs, but from inside sources, it was learned that the Waitt & Bond cigar business and the properties which are pure real estate investments and are returning good money every year, would alone remain in the possession of the Bond family.

Mrs. Bond, Monday forenoon, forwarded the first statement, which she has made since her husband's death to the newspapers. It was as follows: "My husband was not a suicide. I want that statement denied. It seems as if at such a time as this, people ought not to add to our grief by saying such things. All his friends who really knew him know that the suicide theory is untenable. He had no reason to do such a thing as he says, he was killed by his friends and enemies, but it was a natural death.

For three days before his death he was very much depressed by the terrible things that were being said about him. The criticisms and the talk of those whom he believed to be his friends had been making about his business deals were known to him. His health, which had not been too good recently, was affected by all this and his heart was weakened. I believe he wrote that note when he felt an attack of heart failure coming on. His business was in good condition, but the stress of so many large business deals wore upon him. He was so much a philanthropist and lived his life so much to give pleasure to others that it seems as if they, at least, could deal gently with his memory."

Miss Edith Bond also disclaimed the probability of suicide and said:

"I had a long talk with Dr. Henry C. Low, of Swampscott, who was the first to be called to the house, and he assured me that my father was not a suicide. I urged him to tell me the facts and, if my father committed suicide, to say so. He told me that he and Medical Examiner Pinkham had gone carefully over the case and had agreed that it was not suicide. They account for the note which my father left in his room by the fact that he was perhaps preparing for a bath when taken with an attack of heart trouble, and that he hurriedly seized a paper and pencil and wrote that note.

If he had intended to commit suicide, he would have taken a piece of letter paper, which was handy, and would have written more carefully. His handwriting showed that he was very weak. He also had a pistol in his room, which he kept there in case of burglars and which he would, undoubtably, have used if he had intended suicide. His mental condition was absolutely sound."

Trustee Newell could not tell Monday what would be done with the plans for the Lyric Theatre, which Mr. Bond had planned to erect in Boston. An intimate friend of the deceased asserted that the estate would amount to a considerable fortune when all the affairs are settled, for, although some of the real estate ventures must eventually turn out to be direct losses, he held equities in several good properties – The Oceanside at Magnolia netted a $15,000 profit last year and the outlook this season is far more encouraging.

Certificate of Death
Town of Swampscott, Massachusetts

Certificate of Death
Commonwealth of Massachusetts
Town of Swampscott

County of Essex

The following is a copy from the record of Death in said Town:

Name	Charles Henry Bond
Date of Death	July 3, 1908
Date of Birth	Age 61
Occupation	Cigar Manufacturer
Sex	Male
Single, Married, Widowed or Divorced	Married
Cause of Death	Drowning in Bathtub
Place of Death	Swampscott
Residence	Swampscott
Birthplace	Saugus, MA
Name of Father	Charles Milton Bond
Birthplace of Father	Saugus, MA
Maiden Name of Mother	Mary Ameridge
Birthplace of Mother	Boston, MA
Place of Interment	Mt. Auburn Crematory, Cambridge MA

I, Russell Patten, depose and say that I hold the office of Town Clerk, of the Town of Swampscott, in the County of Essex, and the Commonwealth of Massachusetts; that the Records of Deaths in said Town are in my custody, and that the above is true extract from the Records of Deaths, in said Town as certified by me.

WITNESS my hand and the seal of the said Town of Swampscott, this 28th day of August 2007

Russell Patten

A TRUE COPY ATTEST: Russell Patten, Town Clerk of the Town

Grave of Isabella Bacon Bond

Bond collection

Members of patriotic societies learned with regret of the death of Mrs. Isabella Bacon Bond of 128 Commonwealth Avenue, Boston, and Peace Haven Swampscott. Although, due to ill health, she had been less active in patriotic works, during the past two years, she had already given too much to their cause to be easily forgotten.

Mrs. Bond's interest in patriotic organizations was to be expected, since six of her maternal forbears and a paternal ancestor were enrolled in the American ranks during the Revolution.

She was a member of the board of assistance, Society of Mayflower Descendants, and belonged to the Society of Daughters of Colonial Wars and a charter member of the Paul Revere Chapter, Daughters of the American Revolution, of Boston. She served as its regent from 1804 to 1907. During that time, she founded the Signal Lantern

Society, Children of the American Revolution, organizing it in January of 1904. She was vice president general of the National Society, D.A.R. from 1913 to 1914 and national chairman of international relations from 1917 to 1920.

Patriotic work was only one of many interests, however. She was a member of many clubs and was a writer and public speaker. She was a graduate from the department of oratory at the New England Conservatory of Music.

Perhaps this background first inspired her interest in the MacDowell colony at Peterborough, N.H. In 1925, she gave the colony a recreation and entertainment hall to be known as Bond Assembly Hall, in memory of her husband.

In 1966, Mr. Bond's family donated a large portrait size photograph of CHB to the Saugus Public Library. Mr. Bond donated funds to the first library in 1884. The portrait was transferred to the front hall of the Saugus Town Hall and was taken down during the renovations.

The portrait is now located in the Marleah E. Graves Building, formerly known as the Cliftondale School, 54-58 Essex Street, Saugus, MA.

Family Reunion at 128 Commonwealth Avenue, Boston, Mass

128 Commonwealth Avenue

May 1, 1983 - 100th Wedding Anniversary of IBB and CHB

128: Home to me and not a circumferential highway. The house at that time was four stories and a basement, a twenty-six foot wide brown sandstone house on the southerly side of the Avenue, midway between Clarendon and Dartmouth Streets. A twin to the house at 130, it had a long flight of steps to the front door and a short flight to the basement level.

Inside, a partition wall separated the right hand third of the house from the larger two thirds, all the way from the cellar to the roof. On the first floor, the vestibule, front stairway and butler's pantry were on the right; the formal parlor at the front, the reception hall amidships, and the dining room at the rear.

On the second floor the Library and Oriental room were at the front; a sewing room used as a play room, and in later years as quarters for Grandma Bacon, with a bed room was at the right, and a bath was across the hall.

On the third floor was Mother's room and my room as a baby, later Mother's office, and, at the front, two bedrooms for my siblings.

On the fourth floor was Papa's room and a guest room at the front, three servants' rooms at the rear and two baths.

P 1 Memoirs of CLB

Bond collection

Grandson Charles Dailey Bond with memorabilia

Bond Collection

Biography of Charles Dailey Bond

Public service and volunteerism run through many of the Bond veins. Mr. Charles Dailey Bond, grandson of Charles Henry Bond, is no exception. Mr. Bond served three terms as State Senator and chose not to run again in 1990 due to the real estate crisis. The yearly salary for a State Senator at that time was $100.00. Mr. Bond took the position of Director of Workers' Compensation for the State of Vermont until retirement in 2000.

He served as fire chief for eight years and a member of the School Board, five as Chairman.

A note written by Charles Dailey Bond

Our good fortune is clearly the product of the golden leaf. Was it not for tobacco, who knows where any of us would be? When CWMB moved to Cliftondale he went into the snuff business, probably because the Sweetser's were in it. Snuff was popular because while satisfying the nicotine urge it didn't start fires in the hayfields and helped deal with the dusty environment of the textile mills of Lynn, which Saugus abuts. There were many mills and tanneries so there was an excellent market. What got CHB started on cigars is uncertain but IBB tells how he started out.

Henry Waitt lived in Franklin Park, a part of Revere about a mile from Cliftondale. There is a Waitt Lane there today. Apparently as fast as Henry made them, Charlie sold them. CLB once told me that his mother would sometimes accompany CHB as he could close a sale so quickly that they could make a sales trip a pleasure ride. He sold primarily to tobacconists.

Most of us have collected something in the way of Waitt and Bond memorabilia. From the soon to disappear central Artery in Boston, the Waitt and Bond building on Endicott St in the North End is still visible. It is a block from Blackstone Street from which the best-known W&B cigars got their name.

Statement of Waitt and Bond stock certificate

The **Waitt and Bond** stock certificate - not an investment of which I am particularly proud, although it seemed smart in 1961. Its worth today is the paper it is printed on less the cost of the frame!

W&B's share holders were, as I remember it, equally HW and CHB with a small number of shares held by Mr Gonzales, the tobacco buyer in Cuba and by Mr Arthur O.Waterman, a relative of CHB's first wife who was the company accountant. Upon the passing of Mr Waitt, the Waterman family acquired a majority interest in Waitt and Bond. After CHB passed on in 1908 neither family was really active in the management of the company. IBB asked both her sons if they wished to be involved in management but Kenneth wanted to practice law and Lawrence wanted to be a civil engineer. At some point she sold her interest in W&B.

The company suffered bankruptcy during the Depression. After WW II it was acquired and reorganized and acquired R G Sullivan of Manchester NH and Alison Fisher, both small competitors. Ultimately it was acquired by another company and called the Blackstone Cigar Company. Blackstone vanished from the market place as cigars went out of favor.

In 1961 I bought 10 shares of preferred stock for sentimental reasons and the certificate is all that is left.

W&B Share

Bond collection

Obituary of Charles Dailey Bond

Charles Dailey Bond, 85 passed away on Sunday November 5, 2017 at The Cottage Hospital in Woodsville, NH. Charlie made a peaceful transition with his loving wife of 36 years, Marie by his side. Charlie, as he was known to family and friends, was born on March 20, 1932 in Boston, MA. He was the oldest son of C. Lawrence and Barbara (Dailey) Bond. He was raised in Topsfield, MA and attended the local elementary school and The Gunnery School in Washington, CT.

He received his Bachelors degree from Harvard College in 1954. His devotion to his country led to his being commissioned in the U.S. Army as a Lieutenant. In 1954 he served as an artillery officer in the 555th, 546th and 720th Field Artillery Battalions at Fort Lewis Washington until 1956. Charlie attained the rank of Captain prior to the completion of his military service.

Charlie worked for over ten years in personnel to include being the Director of Personnel at Dynamics Research in Stoneham, MA until 1969. He was the owner and manager of the Carroll County Company in North Conway, NH from 1969-72. Charlie was a successful Realtor for over 20 years and 'Bond Associates' negotiated the sale of the 4,000 acre Waumbek property to the U.S. Forest Service in 1978. He worked as the Director of Workman's Compensation Division, Department of Labor in the state of Vermont from 1992-2000.

Charlie was a great believer in public service and encouraged and aided by his wife Marie, served both his community and his state in numerous capacities throughout his life. He served on the White Mountains Regional School Board for 14 years, with five as Chairman. He had a lifetime service as a firefighter in every town he lived in which he loved. He was the Volunteer Fire Chief in Jefferson for eight years. He organized the Jefferson Fireman's Association to encourage volunteerism in others. In addition, he organized the Jefferson Historical Society, reorganized the Jefferson Athletic Association and served as the Director of the White Mountain Festival of the Arts that took place on the grounds of the old Waumbek Hotel in Jefferson.

Charlie was a three term state senator serving district 1 in the New Hampshire state legislature. He was a history buff especially in regards to New England as well as the Civil War. He especially enjoyed researching family genealogy. He had an affinity for Rome and it's history. Even though he was of Scottish, Irish and English ancestry, we always joked that he had the heart of a Roman. When he first visited Rome it was love at first sight.Charlie was an avid mountain climber and completed every possible 'list' including the New Hampshire highest peaks and most of New England's highest.

The Jefferson local was kind and generous. He recently said, "I want it remembered that I really loved humanity" as evidenced by how he lived his life. Survivors include his wife Marie (Rogers) Bond of Jefferson and children, son C. Parker Bond and his wife Ann Marie of Alabaster, Alabama, Geoffrey Bond and his wife Hilary of Wayne, PA, Eliza Crescentini and her husband Marco of Holyoke, MA, Joshua Bond and his wife Leann of East Nausau, NY and Rachel Bond of Oakland, CA, brother Nathaniel and his wife Beth Bond of Glenburne, ME and many grandchildren, nieces and nephews. He was predeceased by his sister Priscilla and brothers Alan Bond of Rochester, VT and Jonathan Bond of Orr's Island, ME. Servies 11/11/at 11 AM.at Jefferson Town Hall. Potluck reception following, please bring your favorite dish.

Waitt and Bond Building, Boston, MA 2019

(jkj)

(Note: On November 29, 2019, the Boston Herald reported that the Waite and Bond building, once housing the largest cigar manufacturers in the Unitied States, will be converted into Condo's.)

Chapter III

THE LASTING LEGACY OF CHARLES HENRY BOND

The Cliftondale/Bond School

Mr. Charles Henry Bond, multimillionaire, philanthropist, and cigar manufacturer, was born in Saugus, Massachusetts and lived in Saugus for many years and then off to Boston with summers in Swampscott, Massachusetts.

Up until 1899, Mr. Bond resided in a beautiful home in Cliftondale and was always ready to assist the public projects in Saugus. He was one of the original members of the Saugus Water Board, was President of the Cliftondale Library Association to whom he donated many books, Trustee of the Saugus Library, and always offered great financial assistance to the Charles H. Bond Camp, Sons of Veterans, Saugus, MA.

The Bond home in Swampscott, "Peace Haven" was noted for the splender of the entertainment given there, and every season several concerts were given at which artists who had Mr. Bond's patronage repaid him somewhat for his philanthropy.

Among the summer colonists at Swampscott, Mr. Bond was known as the 'Macacnas of the North Shore'. Through his aid, several young women attained fame as singers, for whenever a voice interested him and the owner could not afford to cultivate it, he paid her expenses for training in this country and abroad.

Among them were Geraldine Farrar, May Pendergast, and Ada Chambers of New York. He allowed them $100 a month for their living expenses and gave them a thorough training by the best European Masters.

In 1893, Mr. Bond donated two properties on Essex Street. The first at 50 Essex Street – the Cliftondale Congregational Church and 54-58 Essex Street, the Cliftondale School now known as the Marleah Elizabeth Graves (MEG) School.

In 2007, several residents leased the school building from the Town and organized the MEG Foundation, a non-profit group sponsoring school concerts, plays, fundraisers benefiting local charities, and host to several althetic programs to name a few.

It is interesting to note that, although Mr. Bond has long since passed, his passion to support the arts and other town wide events continues to this day at the MEG!

Original Blue Prints

(Courtesy of Massachusetts Archives)

Saugus needs a new school

Mr. Penn Varney, born in Wolfeboro, New Hampshire on November 15, 1854, and a well-known architect, was hired by the Town of Saugus to design the Bond School to be located on Essex Street. Mr. Varney's business was located at 44 Central Square, Lynn, MA. His many projects include Lynn Classical High School, the Melrose Public Library, and the Sanford Maine Town Hall, to name a few.

To assist the Town in the project, Charles Bond and Benjamin Waitt donated the property for the school. Because of their generous gift, it was agreed among the townsfolk that the new school would be named the Bond School upon completion. Unfortunately, an article was submitted to name the school the Cliftondale School.

Original Minutes taken from the Saugus Town Meeting 1893

The 'no name' plaque

Town Meeting Member Charles F. Fyfe offered a motion to reconsider but it did not pass. Strangely enough the plaque where the name was supposed to be inserted was left blank and there never was a sign on the property stating the name 'Cliftondale School.'

The school building was completed in approximately 14 months. The building featured four large classrooms, two lobbies, extra-large windows facing the east to capture sunlight, slate blackboards imported from Italy, a full basement, hand carved woodwork, and two magnificent staircases. In the fall of 1884, it opened for neighborhood school children.

School completed 1894

Bond collection

Three classes 1912

Students on front steps of School

1. Leland Coombs; 2. Gordon Binney; 3. Gladys Pulsifer; 4. Tom Norris; 5. Annie Raddin; 6. Gladys Smith; 7. Doris Nahlswish; 8. Laura Weatherbee; 9. Viola Campbell; 10 Addie Carter; 11 Alice Smith; 12. ?; 13 Clement Smith; 14 Elise Hatch; 15 Jess Mansfield; 16 Hazel Fisher; 17 Lacy Briendy; 18 Tallmadge Mackenzie; 19 Guy Fife; 20 Edna Hill; 21 Blanch Batchelder; 22 Margery Tucker ; Amy Allerton; 24 Teacher Miss A. C. Chase.

Bond collection

Cliftondale School Diploma

Charles A. Williams – Grammar School Diploma June 21, 1907
The Williams family lived on School Street

(Great Grandmother Emma J. (Parker, my great, great grandmother) Charles A. Williams a nephew– deceased left all papers, bibles and photos to Emma Parker)

First Grade students – 1933

Mrs. MacVicar taught first grade at the school and gave me this class photo to be included in my story. She passed away several years ago but I received permission from her son, Norman, to include her photograph.

1. Hollis Eaves; 2. Marilyn Pratt; 3. Louise Wood; 4. Nancy Prunier; 5. Arthur Michaelson; 6. Emma Thurlin; 7. Beverly Battman; 8. Calvin Vatcher; 9. Erva Patterson; 10. Shirley Martin; 11. Donald Coombs; 12. Robert Tolman; 13. Elsie Day; 14. Marian Huff; 15. Robert Kane; 16. David Nagle; 17. Marie Czerwonka; 18. Evelyn Stewart; 19. Richard Allen; 20. Ruth Crooker; 21. Frances Sandberg; 22. Arthur Spinney; 23. William Cole; 24. Helen Poole; 25. Donald Reiniger; 26. James Hanlon; 27. Malcolm Blunt; 28. Virginia Binney; 29. Emma Rossetti; 30. James McLaughlin; 31. Muriel Elderkin; 32. Frances Biggart; 33. Robert Moran; 34. Virginia Brown; 35. Antonio Flammia.

(Note: Photo permission courtesy of MacVicar family)

Class at Saugus Town Hall 1939

This picture was taken on 13 April 1939 on the steps of the Town Hall in Saugus. We are fourth grade students and attended the Cliftondale School. The Principal of that school also taught fourth grade. Her name was Mrs. Myra Beckman and she was an excellent teacher.

1st row, L to R
Eleanor Reehill, Vera Jean Fyfe, Janet McLeod Ruth Cassey, Vail Wilkinson, William Callahan, Theresa Nagle, Bayley Mason, Charles Flynn, Alden Neal, Herbert Shah and Grover Parsons.

2nd row, L to R
Elizabeth Brougham, Constance Thulin, Marilyn McLean, Donald Henshel, June Callahan, Arthur Laura, Ada Sweezey, Jack Sampson, George Oxley.

3rd row, L to R
Pat Sheehan, Leonora Aucella, Agnes Chuck, Natalie MacAdoo, Dorothy Biggart, Gertrude Pitman, Eileen Hayes

4th row, L to R
Ethel Bambury Barbara Ludwig, Donald LeBlanc, Dorothy Shepherd, Margaret Carbone, Jacqueline Ellis and Mrs. Myra Beckman

(courtesy of Saugus Advertiser

Cliftondale School Dentist Town Report – 1934

Board of Health Report

BOARD OF HEALTH

Samuel Gillespie
Welcome Goss
Harry W. Merrill

      Permits and licenses issued totaled 644; Plumbing permits 295; milk analysis 57; and dog bites checked totaled 132. Sewer entrance applications approved totaled 34 and investigations of cesspools totaled 186. Slaughtered animals inspected totaled 7. Restaurants and stores were periodically inspected.

      During 1948 there were 192 contagious diseases reported. A total of 1376 home visits were made by the nurse. In cooperation with the State a program for treatment of rheumatic fever patients was maintained. Diptheria prevention clinics were operated and in connection therewith 394 high school students were inoculated. The department has been active in the protection and care of tuberculosis patients.

      The dental clinic was held twice a week and continues to contribute to the present and future health of Saugus children.

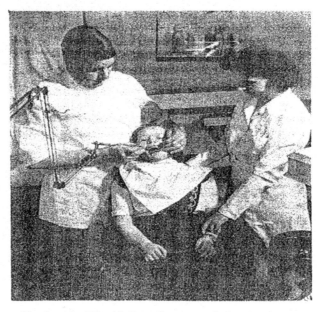

The Board of Health Dental program helps develop the healthy bodies so necessary to house the sound minds of our children.

List of Services - Dr. Robert P. Beckman D.M.D.

BOARD OF HEALTH REPORT

December 31, 1934, Report of Supervisor of the Dental Clinic.

To the Board of Health:

Gentlemen,

I herewith submit my annual report of the Dental Clinic.

Needy children from the first two grades are treated at the clinic. A small fee of $.25 is charged for each visit.

Dental certificates were awarded to the children who had their work completed. A detailed report follows:

Total deciduous extractions	260
Total permanent extractions	20
Total number of fillings	179
Total prophylactic treatments	160
Total refused treatment	5
Total patients	624
Receipts for year	$156.00

Respectfully submitted: Robert P. Beckman, D.M.D., December 27, 1934

Information provided by Janice Jarosz from 1934 Town Report

Robert P. Beckman D.M.D

(From Saugus, MA Town Report 1935)

To this day, many visitors to the Marleah E. Graves School will only peek into the once infamous 'Dentist Office.' A few former students of the school related horror stories remembering their first visit to the office.

I often wondered how the children in the surrounding classrooms dealt with the screams and hollering that must have occurred. It wasn't until I read this report that I learned I also was a 'needy child.' I, along with others, were only five or six when we had our appointments with Dr. Beckman.

I remember holding onto the quarter while walking from the Felton School on Central Street, to 54 Essex Street, then standing in line in the lobby. I don't remember anything else - maybe I was one of those refusing treatment!

(Mrs. Robert Beckman served as principal of the school during this time)

Chapter IV

MEET MISS GRAVES

Miss Marleah Elisabeth Graves 1973

(Courtesy of Saugus Advertiser)

One of the most popular and loving teachers at the Cliftondale School was Miss Marleah Elizabeth Graves who taught the second grade class for over 47 years. Miss Graves was born in the family home in Saugus, MA and lived her entire life there. She graduated from Saugus High School in 1924 and from North Adams Normal School, now North Adams State College, in 1926. Upon receiving her teaching certificate, she returned to Saugus to teach elementary school.

Following two years at the Mansfield School on Lincoln Avenue, Miss Graves moved to the Cliftondale School where she taught second grade beginning in 1932 and retiring in 1975 after 47 years teaching in the Saugus school system.

Miss Graves received several honors during her lengthy career as a much loved and highly respected teacher. She was named as the National Elementary School Teacher of the Year in 1970. She was a lifelong member of the Ivy Club and a member of the Saugus Retired Teachers' Association.

John McCarthy, a student of hers, remembers how she comforted him when his father passed away. John was in the second grade during the Great Depression and each morning Miss Graves greeted him with a welcoming smile and a warm 'hug.' John explained, "It meant so much to me those thoughtful gestures and acts of kindness my favorite teacher gave me during a difficult time in my younger years."

A field Day at Anna Parker Playground

The following 'thank you' notes were written by the second-grade class of Miss Graves. The students all seemed to enjoy the day at Anna Parker playing games and the fun they all shared.

> Dear Cathy Haase
>
> How are you?
>
> Would you like to go to Anapaker today? I hope you would come.
>
> From Julie Cushman

By Julie Cushman

> To Mr. Bogdan
>
> Dear Mr. Bogdan
>
> I had fun at the park and the most fun off all was jumping in the bags
>
> From Susan Contrada
>
> oh tell Mrs. Bogdan thank you for the nich
> ¡l

By Susan Contrada

George Anastos

I like The firestation the best and the library and the game sa\~~se~~ ating

By George Anastos

Timothy Sharp

I had fun at the park yesterday we had lunch and after that we had relay races after that we had refreshments then we went home.

By Tim Sharp

> Patricia Nichols
> had fun at the fire station + the library.
> And the School picnic
> And Mrs. Parker was nice to me + cathy
> And I ma going to

By Patricia Nichols

> Jean Ludwig
> Dear Miss Graves
> I loved the school picnic. I hope you liked it to. Did you?
> I know Mr. and Mrs. Bogdan liked it to.

By Jean Ludwig

> Mr. Bogdan told us how to play good games And I liked them to. Did you ↑ THE END. P.S your the best teacher in the school

Jean Ludwig, page 2

Thank you letter from Miss Graves to Mrs. Shirley Bogdan

> Dear Mr. and Mrs. Bogdan,
> I have been debating whether to send these letters to you or not. However everyone was very appreciative of the good work done by you and many other parents and this is how the youngsters expressed themselves.
> Please accept them in sincere way of saying "thanks". (Also please understand that I still do teach spelling!) My personal thanks to you both.
> Sincerely,
> Marleah Graves.

(Courtesy of Shirley Bogdan)

A fellow teacher writes

By Miss Constance Putnam

It was quite often the case that each classroom held approximately 40-46 students during my tenure in the 1930's and 40's. I was the first-grade teacher and Marleah Graves was not only my colleague, but my best friend as well. We taught on the first floor with our classrooms next to one another and Marleah was the second-grade teacher. If we were assigned a class of less than 40 students, we were both in heaven that year!

As a first-grade teacher, I remember my children as disciplined, well-behaved and respectful, not only of me, but of their parents and fellow students as well. For the most part, students behaved and listened to the teacher but if there was a problem with a student, which was rare, the parents would side with the teacher and exact their own discipline at home.

During my years in college, we were taught that the eyes of a child were not developed fully enough to learn how to read until they reached the age of seven. We did not know about autism at that time and I do not recall anyone getting sick over peanut butter. Few children had asthma and very few of my students required any kind of medication.

As teachers, we did not assign homework to our students until the fourth grade. We believed that youngsters needed fresh air and exercise as much as they needed lessons in the Three R's.

In my teaching career, children were able to attend neighborhood schools where children knew their classmates and neighbors. Most children today do not have that advantage. It must be simply awful to put a young child on a bus and send him or her off to a school in another section of town. It is no wonder why children are so stressed out today.

I have been very fortunate to have lived a long life and to be able to see how well so many of my students turned out. Some of the ones I never expected to make it in the world became the most successful ones of all - one just never knows the real potential of a young student!

Another advantage to living a long life has been the opportunity to meet many of my former students in our adult years. It is such a joy to talk to them about their elementary school days and the wonderful times we shared together at the Cliftondale School.

Courtesy of Constance Putnam

My early memories

By William (Bill) McAdoo

I attended the first though the fourth grade, September, 1937 to June, 1941, at the Cliftondale School, now known as the Marleah E. Graves School.

Every Monday our parents would give us five cents to give to the teacher to buy a sugar cookie or three Ritz crackers to go with the daily government sponsored milk program.

One Monday I went into Kimball's Mom and Pop store and bought five cents worth of penny candy of which I gave Joe Gamage, the school janitor, a piece of my candy as he helped us cross Essex Street to the school. That taught me about sharing. Now I didn't have the five cents for the Ritz Crackers so it was a long week with just the milk!

Miss Graves was my second-grade teacher and I loved her for her kindness, her true affection for students and her teaching skills. From her we learned much more than the three R's.

Today, I'm very happy to be a board member of the MEG Foundation. It is a fulfilling addition to my life because the board members are a wonderful group. When I first got my key to the school building, I would go in and reminisce.

My Memories of the Cliftondale School
1952 –1955

By Mary Dunlop

I have many fond memories of my first three years at the Cliftondale School. It was a 'neighborhood school' which meant that everyone walked to school.

My route started with a stroll through Cliftondale Square down as far as "Shorty's" gas station. There I was always met by a policeman, either Bill McKinney or Roy Bucchiere, who made sure that we all got across Lincoln Avenue safely. They knew all of us and would always have something special to say to each one of us.

My route continued along "Hanson Chevrolet," by the principal's house, the church and finally onto the playground. Because the playground wasn't paved and was very rocky, I had chronic scabs on my knees. I know my mother thought I would never have normal knees!

Back then every girl wore a dress, and slacks were only worn under your dress on cold winter days and they were removed as soon as we got into school and hung in the coatroom.

My principal was Mrs. Myra Beckman, who we were all afraid of. She taught the fourth grade and her husband was a dentist. He had a big dental chair in the front room of the school. I remember hearing the kids crying!

My first-grade teacher was Miss Anthony and Miss Marleah Graves was my second-grade teacher. Miss Graves was my all-time favorite teacher. She was a gentle and caring teacher with a soft voice but was firm in her own way.

I remember her washing out a boy's mouth with soap at the sink in the hallway. When the first-grade teacher needed to leave her room, she would ask Miss Graves if one of her students would go in and watch her students. I was the one she usually picked!

Our desks were made of wood, had slanted tops that lifted, ink wells, and were anchored to the floor. We could either eat lunch at the school at our desks or go home for lunch because there was no cafeteria then.

I remember the milkman bringing a wooden crate filled with cartons of milk into our classroom each morning and setting it on the floor in the corner. I happened to be right near the corner so that is probably why I remember it so vividly.

My second-grade experience being taught by Miss Graves left a very positive imprint on me. My third-grade teacher was Miss Doris Hart.

When we found out that the "Sweetser School" was no longer going to be the junior high and that it would be used for grades four, five, and six, we were all excited because we wouldn't have to have Mrs. Beckman!

As I left the Cliftondale School for the last time, I had no idea what a positive impact my experiences there would have on my life.

I am so thankful for the wonderful memories and will always cherish them.

(Courtesy of Mary Dunlop)

Politics way back then!

By Larry Seavers SHS Class of 1962

I was born in Lynn Hospital and spent my first few years in Lynn. In 1950, our family settled in at 8 Smith Road, Saugus, MA and I was enrolled at the Cliftondale Elementary School, second grade.

Our class loved recess – the best part of school. Our pals would get together, lock arms and march around the playground chanting, "Anyone in our way gets a 5-cent boot." I don't remember anyone getting in our way.

Miss Graves was my second-grade teacher and she helped me pass into the third grade. It had been a difficult time changing from the first grade in Lynn to Saugus as I was a 'cutup' and Miss Beckman said I should be buggy whipped!

I remember Principal Myra Beckman with her leather strap. When called to her office she would fiddle with it, but I never remember her using it.

In 1952, it was the Presidential election time and we were all interested in it. So much so that we would again lock arms and recite the famous phrase at that time – "We like IKE." General Dwight D. Eisenhower, a Republican, was running against Adlai Stevenson, a Democrat.

One afternoon at recess one rare, but very brave Democrat in the crowd stood up in front of us and yelled STEVENSON!!!! It was Danny O'Donnell!!!

(Courtesy of Larry Seavers)

Miss Graves in her classroom

(Courtesy of Saugus Advertiser)

My memories of Miss Graves

By Tom Sheehan

"Miss Graves was slim, had short hair, wore a long skirt, flat shoes, and was very nice."

Those words come from a classmate by the name of Theresa, in Miss Graves' second grade class in 1936, I believe knowing how some memories reach to be cast in bronze again or get lost at the wayside. Miss Marleah Graves was never cast aside or lost. She lingers forever.

Recess in those years was a burst from the steps of the school into the schoolyard, playing tag, tossing a ball, the girls at hopscotch or jump rope, excited, lit up, coming into their personal beauty the years took by the and embellished. And she was always present, her eyes alert, her care evident a real lady in the mix of life. She was lithe and dexterous and promised to live forever, or so it seemed, and she made a great run at it, as the years proved.

After the first recess came lunch, a run for home and crackers and Campbell's tomato soup and a noon voice on the radio, with ads for Barber Sol, sung by Singing Sam. We lived on the third floor flat, just past the Hanson's Garage and just before Myrtle Street that went off to the right as Lincoln Avenue went downtown toward North Revere, and after Louis Gordon's Taylor Shop and Joe Laura's Barber Shop.

The rush back to school for the afternoon session was energetic, as though she was always calling us back for more nourishment, curiosity, a sense of time hanging in the universe about the Cliftondale School, at her demand.

Of course, you know who was responsible for having such an impact on a young life…the sweet lady the kind lady, the energetic lady, the slim lady who pushed us, drew work and hope from us, watched as we grew from that second grade class, moving on, her life constant in that one place for more than three quarters of a century…Miss Marleah E. Graves, who indeed was slim, who wore short hair, long skirts, flat shoes, and lives yet beside, in, among, about a red brick school some may think is cool and aged, and yes, so are the memories.

The reconnaissance of stars and rockets, take your pick as you look upon a dark night, began on the fourth of July in the schoolyard of the old Cliftondale School, somewhere in the mid 1930's. The morning was as soft as a fresh bun, as warm, air floating upward, moving with the smell of burnt cork or punk as smoky as a compost pile from the debris night had collected.

There were spent rockets in Essex Street gutters, on Myrtle Street, about the green, towering treed Cliftondale Square, the clutter of half-burnt rockets one afire in the sky of the previous night. They had given darkness a new dimension of light and sound about our school with explosions of flares too bright to look at. It was as if the sun had delayed departure for the heart of our celebration, friction of them in the measure as silent as Indians in the past on these same fields and paths at flint and rock, above the place where Staff Road would come along years later, and run over-hill to School Street.

It happened even as children younger than me went about the ways and adjoining roads and green lawns collecting what had fallen on Jackson Street and Bond Place and Smith Road and the Cinder Path off Baker Hill, those expended shafts of ultra-excitement. They rolled them into the quivers of their hands, held them against their noses smelling the residue of sky-reaching powder such short fires had given off while the night was black. When clutched in their hands a match seemed re-applied in secret and the celebration blaze began anew for those without money to buy their own pyrotechnics from the stand on Jackson Street, beside what was to become George's Barber Shop.

Depression Days did this.

They might see again the blue-red and orange-green flames loosed by this completion exceeding much I had seen on the holiday eve, these young scavengers, young army of excitement seekers fresh as a wind adrift on the dawn. With them was never-forgotten young pal Charlie who was lost later in the swirl of adulthood. He moved away, though I remember him still as he sat directly in front of me in Miss Graves' second grade class, one of the searchers in life, early afflicted with infantile paralysis who somehow, with determination and courage, became a fierce running back elsewhere from Stackpole Field many of us came to know in our own short times there.

I am sure that Miss Graves remembers him too, even on another holiday season, for that day she stood across the street watching us on a day without school, her attention never faltering.

Years later, Mr. Sheehan wrote about the third-floor porch of that three decker:

Searching for Mushrooms and Trolley Cars, (Amanita Colyptraderma and Electric Street Cars

They came out of West Lynn or East Saugus years ago, dark mushroom seekers, with their long-pieced poles, their own language whose word for amanita, to the initiate, would tell where their roots began, whether they were Florentine, Roman or islander, Piana di Cartania. They might say *Cocoli, Coloni or Coccori*, the delicacies growing thirty or forty feet up on the great elms in the circled green of Cliftondale Square, those huge sky-reaching elms that fell to the hurricanes of '38 or Carol in the '50's, finally to the toll of traffic demanding the green circle be cut down to size.

Once, in a thick fog, on my third porch floor, the mist yet memorable, I remember thinking the elms were *Gardens in the Clouds*. I felt a bloom rise in me; a taste fills my mouth.

They don't come for amanita anymore because the elms have all gone, those lofty gardens, those mighty furrowed limbs; now shrubs and bushes stand in their place you can almost see over.

Nor do I see street cars come anymore from Lynn into Cliftondale Square. They say the old yellow ones and orange ones, high black-banded ones red-roofed ones, real noisy ones, ones long-electric-armed at each end, the one off the Lynn-Saugus run, are in Brazil or Argentina or the street car museum in Kennebunkport, Maine, quiet now forever as far as we are concerned, those clanging, rollicking machines that flattened pennies on the tracks so good that Old Abe became a complete mystery, or the Indian Chief, him and his background, became as flat and as charmless as his reservation.

From my porch high on the square, I'd watch think long poles extending men's arms, needles of poles they'd fit together, as they reached for the white-gray knobs growing in cloudy limbs. They wore red or blue kerchiefs around thick necks, lie Saturday's movie cowboys if you could believe it, as if any moment they could slip them over their faces and hide out in such bright disguises. They'd cut or tap loose the amanita, see it fall slowly end over end, like a field goal or a touchdown's point-after, down out of the upper limbs, cutting a slowest curve and halved orbit, and they'd swish butterfly nets to catch the aerial amanita, or *Cocoli*, as it might be; or their women, in kerchiefs and drawn in and almost hidden away, faces almost invisible, with an upward sweep of gay aprons would catch the somersaulting fungi, the amanita colyptraderma, or being from Piana di Cartania, calling out its name *Coconi* or *Coccori*.

Oh, Mediterranean's rich son airing itself across the green grass of Cliftondale Squire, Brahminnville being braced, uplifted.

I was never privy to know their roots, their harsh voyages, to know where they landed and why, and now their sounds are lost forever, their voices across the square, the gay and high-pitched yells setting a brazen mish on Cliftondale, their glee as a soft while clump of fungi went loose from its roost, coming down to net, swung apron, or quick hat as if a magician worked on stage in the squire, heading *for Russula Delica, Cocoli Trippati, Veal Scaloppine, Mushroom Trifolati, Risotto Milanaise,* or plain old *Brodo dei Funjghi.*

All these years later I know the heavens of their kitchens, the sweet blast front hallways could lose, how sauce pots fired up your nose, how hunger could begin on a full stomach when Mrs. Forti cooked or Mrs. Tedeschi or Mrs. Tura way over there at the foot of Vinegar Hill feeding her gang of seven and their guests.

And I grasp for the clang-clang of the trolley cars, the all-metallic timpani of their short existence, the clash of rods and bars stretching to the nth degree, of iron wheel on iron rail echoing to where we car-waited up the line with fire crackers or torpedoes quick explosions and the whole jangling car shaking like a vital Liberty Ship I'd come to know intimately years later on a dreadful change of tide.

How comfortable now would be those hard-wooden seats whose thick enamel paint peeled off by a fingernail as I left her initials and mine on the back of a seat, wondering if today someone in Buenos Aires or Brasilia rubs an index finger across the pair of us that has not been together for more than sixty years. But somehow, in the gray air today, in a vault of lost music carrying itself from the other end of town, that pairing continues, and the amanita, with its dark song-rich gardeners, though I taste it rarely these days, and the shaky ride the streetcars, for all of a nickel on an often-early evening, softest yet in late May, give away the iron cries and, oh that rich Italiana.

Once a sheer edge of moonlight, a reflection hung in my mind of a whole night's vision, the smell and the sound of it all, the touch of things as they were.

Of course, you know who was responsible for such a turn of events, such a twist to the future, such an impact on a young life…the sweet lady, the kind lady, the energetic lady, the slim lady who pushed us, drew work and hope from us, watched us as we grew from that second grade class, moving on, her life constant in that one place for more than three quarters of a century...Miss Marleah E. Graves, who indeed was slim, who wore short hair, long skirts, flat shoes, and lives yet, beside, in among, about a red brick school some may think is cool and aged, and yes, so are the memories.

(Courtesy of Tom Sheehan)

Miss Graves - More than Just a Teacher

By Carole Andrews, PTO President 1975

Miss Graves was more than just an excellent teacher to my five boys and one daughter. They loved her for her kindness and warmth throughout their early and impressionable years, thinking of her as you would a 'favorite aunt' as well.

Oftentimes they would stop by her house, after school hours, to say hello or to show her something they had done. When I found out they were visiting her, I called to apologize but she told me she loved those visits and always welcomed them.

Miss Graves treated my children as if they were a part of her family to which I am eternally grateful and when she retired, the Patents Teachers Organization hosted a 'Tea' in her honor – a proper testimony to an elegant and gracious lady.

Note: All six children of the late Richard and Carole's family, Richard, Kevin, Brian, Darryl, Dana and Mark continue to volunteer to the preservation of the building in their mother's name. Sister Patricia passed away while in the 3rd grade, 1967, from an automobile accident.

(Courtesy of the Andrews sons)

Miss Marleah Graves – a Great Teacher

By Dr. Robert Munnelly
Superintendent of Schools
1964-1970

I remember Marleah Graves as a wonderful second grade teacher at the Cliftondale School. She was always kind and had a soft and quiet way of teaching young children.

The teaching of reading was her strength. My contact with her was in my role as curriculum co-coordinator for all elementary schools in Saugus and I visited her classroom on a regular basis. My special assignment was to help the teachers upgrade their science and mathematics experiences of the youngsters. Marleah Graves was always interested in providing the best instruction for her children. She was an active participant in what, at the time, was new learning for her.

What made her a great teacher was her own desire to learn.

(Courtesy of son Chris Munnelly)

My Memories of Miss Graves

By Jean (McCarthy) Soulios

I don't remember much about the first grade other than my teacher, Miss Piranesi, had dark hair and seemed very young. I remember how sometimes she needed to sit some of the more boisterous boys in the corner when they misbehaved.

When I walked into my classroom on the first day of the second grade, I officially met Miss Graves – my new teacher. She was a trim and soft-spoken lady. Her hair was gray, but her face was still very young looking. She wore her hair curled under in a soft page boy, parted on the side and held in place by a barrette or Bobbie pins.

During my days with Miss Graves I noticed that she would often wear an open cardigan over her top on most days and I think I remember that she would wear a pearl necklace on special occasions. Her manner was always subdued, and her voice was soft spoken and very nurturing.

I remember that Miss Graves very seldom used the corner seat for discipline. She liked to read to us, and the class paid attention when she did.

We brought our lunch to school every day in either a brown sandwich bag or a special lunchbox. There were coatrooms right outside the classroom where our lunches were kept until the bell rang for lunch.

We went outside for recess after our lunch and played in the paved parking lot. Every other day or so, Miss Graves was on lunch duty and that was when she could be the most stern if you were getting too rambunctious. Amazingly, she always seemed to have a way of keeping order without raising her voice!

Looking back and remembering her style and grace, I realized that Miss Graves had a refined upbringing.

Submitted Jeanne (McCarthy) Soulios

My favorite teacher

By Joseph McCarthy

Miss Graves was my second-grade teacher at the Cliftondale School. One day I walked up to her desk and asked her if she would marry me when I grew up. I don't remember what her response was but that was how important she was to me.

She was a very special teacher.

(Courtesy of Joseph McCarthy)

Saugus School Committee honors Miss Graves

(Courtesy of Saugus Advertiser)

The Saugus School Committee honored Miss Marleah E. Graves at a banquet in her honor. A plaque was unveiled naming the school library the Marleah E. Graves Library. Mrs. Elaine Manoogian Espindle was the presenter of two books to the Marleah E. Graves Library.

The P.T.O., both past and present, are grateful to the many people who helped make this Retirement Party so successful. The Refreshment Table was attractively set in seasonal motif. Floral decorations were through the courtesy of Petrie Florist.

Marleah Graves honored

(Courtesy of Saugus Advertiser)

P.T.O Officers, both past and present, are shown with Miss Graves as she cuts her lovely cake. Mesdames Shirley Bogdan, Janice Amabile, Barbara Fee, Ann Barzani, Guest of Honor, Miss Graves, P.T.O. President Carole Andrews, Hazel Alcott and Toni Gillis.

Standing in her o' so familiar room at the Cliftondale School, Miss Marleah E. Graves, greeted her many friends and former pupils at a Retirement Party held in her honor on Tuesday evening.

It seemed like only yesterday that Miss Graves greeted her first room of second grade pupils back in 1930. And Tuesday evening she once again was on the receiving end.

On a scroll appropriately worded for the occasion, were written the many friends' and students' signatures in the finer adult script along with the wandering, half printed, half written names of her more recent students. Over two hundred in all.

An arrangement of dried fall flowers was given by the Ivy Club of the Cliftondale Congregational Church, a bouquet of tea roses by a former student, an overnight tote suitcase by the children of the Cliftondale School, planters, remembrances, gifts and many cards. A corsage of yellow mini mums from the P.T.O. was also presented to Miss Graves.

School renamed

(Photo Janice K. Jarosz)

Chapter V

Cliftondale School closed

jkj

Mr. John Burns, Saugus High School, submitted the following:

Mrs. Joan Curley served as the last principal at the Cliftondale School before it closed in 1980. She divided her time between the Cliftondale School and Sweetser School as principal.

Teachers employed at the school in its final year were:

Ann Wilson - First Grade; Anna Stella – Second Grade; Gerry MacCuish – Third Grade; Bruce Waybright – Fourth Grade.

(From the Town of Saugus Annual Report 1981)

Schools demolished

For the next few years, as five other elementary schools were demolished, the Cliftondale School remained empty. Occasionally, questions were asked about the building; some wanted it demolished to allow for a public parking lot; and several developers eyed it as a possible conversion into senior housing or private apartments.

At one point, the town leased out the property to North Shore Consortium with a 10-year lease. Consortium officials subdivided two classrooms, one on the first floor and one of the second floor. They also put steel doors in several rooms. After the lease was up, they were required to return the building to its original state, but they never did.

The Saugus police and fire departments stored equipment in the basement; the Civil Defense department held meetings there off and on, and beds were placed in the upstairs classroom for emergency use. But because there was no heat, the building was idle most of the time, especially during winter months.

Perhaps it was the offers made by several local developers that caused the town to take another look at the school. But that new interest also alerted several Saugus citizens to look at it as well!

A gathering of supporters!

A group of Saugus citizens gathered at the Marleah E. Graves former 2nd grade classroom one bright and sunny morning in 2007. No minutes were kept but those in attendance brought forth the first of many ideas and proposed projects 'setting the table' in launching the plans to save the school.

'Mapping out a plan'

At another 'meeting of the minds' several town officials attended along with others interested in learning the status of the building. At that second meeting a few town officials expressed regret but conceded that the school was too far gone to be able to be resurrected. They offered several other options the first being to sell the building to someone who would re-purpose it into condominiums; a second idea was to demolish it and turn it into a public parking lot for the merchants of Cliftondale.

The meeting lasted a few hours and at the conclusion, a majority of those in attendance reaffirmed their position to launch a reconstruction movement. The supporters determined that the building was structurally sound and worth saving, and it was agreed to establish the first Board of Directors consisting of Marilyn Carlson, Janice Jarosz, Ruth Swanson, Maryann Taylor, John Smolinsky, Michael LaVecchia, Cam Cicolini, Rosemary DeGregorio and Leo Nicole.

A new life

Thursday, August 9, 2007 • Saugus Advertiser • Page 3

A new life for Cliftondale School

The new officers of the Marleah Graves Foundation, the group that will oversee the transformation of an old elementary school into a community meeting place, include (seated l to r): Janice Jarosz, president; Ruth Swanson, clerk; and treasurer Anthony Eovine (back row, second from right). Attending the signing ceremony were (back row, l to r) Selectmen Peter Rossetti Jr. and Michael Serino, (Eovine) and Selectman Stephen Horlick. Absent from photo is the new Vice President John Smolinsky.

(Courtesy of the Saugus Advertiser)

The Marleah Elizabeth Graves Foundation Board

The newly formed board met several times each week at the school mapping out a priority plan as so many issues required immediate attention; no functioning heating system, broken windows throughout, graffiti all over the walls, peeling paint, pigeons roosting in the eaves, and the most important concern of all was – where are we ever going to get financing to do anything!!!

Realizing that, of course, nothing could be accomplished without funding, the newly formed organization came up with a plan. A brochure was designed by Ann Hadley of JC Marketing, Wakefield, MA explaining our goals and the need for financial help. A mass mailing of the brochure was sent throughout the town and the response was overwhelming!

The Saugus Advertiser and Lynn Item newspapers published informative articles in our efforts to rehab the building Those articles played an integral part in the success of fundraising efforts.

MEG members Rosemary DeGregorio, Leo Nickole, Janice Jarosz, Senator Thomas McGee, Selectman Peter Rossetti, MEG members Edward Carlson, Ruth Swanson, Don Armstrong and Marilyn Carlson met and took up a fundraising effort to purchase windows throughout the building.

Should the Marleah Graves Building (Cliftondale School) Be Used for a Kabuki Theatre?

Saugus Advertiser August 15, 2010

By Peter Manoogian

100 years ago, Saugus had 13 schools. The concept of the "large" elementary school had yet to be thought of. Saugus, like so many New England towns, seemed to have neighborhood schools on every corner. The Felton, Sweetser, Armitage, North Saugus, Cliftondale, Roby, Ballard and the Emerson come to mind. After Proposition 2 1/2 came in 1980, Saugus closed many schools. Well-connected developers were able to buy two of these buildings and turn them into commercial (North Saugus) or residential condos (Emerson). We were supposed to get a playground in North Saugus along with the "bid" price.

Maybe someday. Other schools or school sites were used for public purposes. The Sweetser School site and the Armitage are now used for public housing. The Felton School site is now the home of our beautiful senior center. The Roby School became the school administration building. One school that bucked the trend was the Cliftondale School. Built in 1894, it was originally known as the Bond School after a prominent Saugus family. The name was changed by town meeting after what Atherton refers to as "an unfortunate controversy in connection with it."

By 1985 the Selectmen, except Janette Fasano, were determined to sell off the Cliftondale School. Selectman Hoffman's close friend Joseph Carter of Carter & Towers Engineering (the C.D.M. of back then) put in his bid proxy of "$1.00 over the highest bid." As I recall that would have been $126,001.00.

When the article came to town meeting, we stopped it cold. Town meeting supported my amendment to form the "Cliftondale School Leasing Committee" which consisted of me, Ellen Faiella, Diane VanNest, and Ed Carlson. We completed our report within one year. We pointed out to town meeting the historic nature of the building. We explained how it was one of the best examples of Romanesque architecture on the North Shore. We pointed out that when the building was constructed America was in the midst of its imperial ventures.

The building was constructed as a sentinel, as an outpost, with arch windows and darkened lintels underneath to make it seem more imposing than its size. The bell tower was higher to provide watch. The patterned slate roof is a work of art in and of itself. If you can, stand on the sidewalk across the street and look at the roof and the chimneys.

We held an open house for the townspeople and pointed these things out. It was a great committee and Moderator Clayton Trefry acknowledged the report as "one of the best he had seen come before town meeting." The five of us convinced town meeting NOT to sell the building and to ask the town manager to "lease the building." Norman Hansen was the town manager at that time. He asked us to continue to help leasing the building. We were able to engage a lease with Shore Collaborative for some $1500.00 a month. They would maintain the building and not disturb the woodwork or the tin ceilings.

In the 1990s, I filed an article to rename the building after the teacher Marleah Graves. Her extended family, which included the owners of Star Market, paid for the bronze plaque you now see on the building. We designed the plaque and awarded the contract to Sheehan Monuments of Lynn, MA. I thought at the time that if the building was named after a woman who taught so many Saugus youth, who would dare want to defile this treasure for a quick buck? I am not sure when Shore left, perhaps 2000 to the 2002 range, but when they did, the building fell vacant. Soon rumblings began again to "sell the building" or worse, a suggestion by the Cliftondale Merchants, "to tear it down and make it a parking lot."

That is when Janice Jarosz stepped up to the plate and re-discovered the special nature of this building. With the cooperation of the town manager, she was able to clean it up, raise some funds and get others involved. On August 27, 2007 she officially formed the MEG Foundation after receiving the blessings of the selectmen and the manager. Since that time her group has worked tirelessly to restore the building. They have raised and spent some $300,000.00 to replace the heating system, the windows, etc.

Although Janice has "constructed the frame," she is still "working on the picture." She knows she needs a revenue stream and stable, appropriate uses, such as non-profits, theater and arts related activities. With her motivational skills and a board of energetic and selfless individuals assisting her, I have no doubt that the MEG Foundation will be successful, and the building will be with Saugus for another century at least!

Within the last few months a controversy has erupted. The school department and the town manager are bickering over who controls the vacant school buildings that include the Ballard, the Evans, and yes, the Marleah Graves. Although Supt. Langlois prevailed in regaining the Ballard, the manager is not flying a white flag on the issue of "control." He claims he has an opinion from town counsel John Vasapolli, indicating such. The school department has their attorney claiming that the buildings were never officially relinquished to the town. In one letter the school department attorney specifically cites the Graves building and does not mention the others. This letter is being used by the town manager to claim that the school department wants the Graves building.

Of course, without context, Janice would assume that the school department is gunning for her building. The MEG directors are concerned about potential donations if such a cloud is hanging over the building. Selectman Steve Horlick is now involved in the controversy. As I See It, this is nothing but more Saugus Kabuki Theater - high drama, with never a happy ending. On one side you have a school department determined to maintain autonomy and break the feudal arrangement that town hall has had over them for years.

On the other side you have town hall that has a wary eye on the actions of the school department. Sooner than later elected policy makers should straighten out this mess and allow the MEG Foundation to continue its great work. The school committee can maintain their claim by simply voting to "release control" of the Graves building. Take a lesson from John Marshall in Marbury V Madison. When you act on something, you forever claim the right to act.

(Courtesy of Peter Manoogian)

Spiritual whispers from the school

As 'whispered' to Janice K. Jarosz - 2010

I bring you greetings from the 'Spirit' of the Marleah E. Graves School, formerly known as the Cliftondale School - originally named the Bond School. For reasons unbeknownst to me, the town reneged on its promise to name me the Bond School and never thanked or honored Mr. Bond for his generous donation.

The Cliftondale area of town was growing by leaps and bounds and to accommodate new families, in 1893 town fathers approved plans to build a new school on Essex Street. I was about to become a reality! Mr. Charles H. Bond, a successful businessperson in Cliftondale and a generous benefactor, donated his property to the town that same year and Grover Cleveland was our President.

Mr. Penn Varney of Lynn, MA designed 'me' and the construction was completed within 16 months. Granite came down from Vermont, bricks were made in Essex County, and slate blackboards shipped in from Italy. So smart were these craftsmen as the classrooms were designed with large windows to greet the sun each day for both heat and light as I was not yet introduced to Thomas Edison.

It took a little over a year to complete the project and in 1894 my doors opened; I welcomed young children from grades one to four who lived in the neighborhood. For many years my walls witnessed the laughter and lessons of thousands of children in my classrooms – I served as the home of dedicated and loving teachers; I survived many epidemics, wars and poverty and I stood in amazement witnessing the fortitude and determination of students learning about The Swiss Family Robinson, Black Beauty and memorizing Psalm 24, and I beamed with pride when the American Flag was raised on 16 holidays, one being Mother's Day.

Each year the town awarded prizes to students who developed the best vegetable gardens and at the end of each school year, Mr. Bond held a Recitation Program awarding prizes for the best presentations. For over 75 years I helped in the education of neighborhood children of Cliftondale sometimes with 40 students per class – students who lived close to one another, who walked together and who grew up together.

But by 1973, neighborhood elementary schools became outdated and five were demolished to make way for new buildings and new concepts in education. By the grace of God, the Roby and I survived - but just barely. Considered old and outdated by many, my doors were shut to any further educational purpose and for the next few years various groups met in my rooms, but no one stayed very long. The heat was eventually shut off and I was now totally all alone suffering both mentally and physically for the next several, long years.

A little ray of sunshine came through my shuttered windows just when I was ready to give up any hope of ever being restored. A group of citizens formed a committee to study the potential use of me. The Board of Selectmen appointed Peter Manoogian, Diane Van Nest, Ellen Burns, Edward Carlson and Ellen Faiella to complete a Needs Assessment of the building. Thankfully, their study determined that the building should remain with the town as they felt it was a valuable resource not to be demolished, sold or given away. This group took the first big step in saving me.

The news came as a relief to me and a 10-year lease was granted by the Town to North Shore Consortium. This group operated a private school but, after the lease was up, I was left alone again; locked up and shut off from the world.

In late 2007, that all changed once again and I believe that my benefactor, Mr. Charles H. Bond, although gone for many years, quietly played a part in the 'urban renewal' of me. For some unknown and unremembered reason, several Saugonians visited me one day and after a tour they realized what I knew all along – I was an asset just waiting to be productive to the town!

And so, for the past three years, they have voluntarily donated their time and energy to fulfill the dream that Mr. Bond had over one hundred years ago. In order to realize the integrating back into the community, it has been you, the townsfolk, the former students, the town officials and the business community who have made that dream a reality.

You came with your donations, elbow grease and moral support. You also brought with you renewed hope and a vision that I could be of value to the community once again.

While the original group dreamed of restoring me to a useful and functioning purpose – it was you, the ones who came full of ideas of how it could be done. It's because of your faith and belief in the group meeting three years ago, that we are all here together today enjoying the beauty of a building grateful to be treasured, productive and loved once again.

Update on the Marleah E. Graves School

The renovation of the Marleah Graves Building, also known as the Cliftondale School, has continued despite the cold, winter weather. Town Manager Andrew Bisignani has been guiding us along the way and his support and encouragement has been the mainstay of the project.

Built in 1894, the Cliftondale School is now known as the Marleah Graves Building and is located at 54-58 Essex Street, just out of Cliftondale Square on the way to Route One. Various contractors have been meeting with architect Michael LaVecchia to discuss proposals to update and restore the building for public use. The first boost the MEG Foundation received was a grant by the Essex National Heritage Commission in the summer of 2008. Then a very successful capital campaign was initiated in which residents and businesses in Saugus made generous contributions to underwrite the restoring and updating of this architectural gem and town treasure for the benefit of the Saugus community.

Last fall the original oak front and back entry doors were completely restored and recently both porch roofs were repaired by Stanley Roofing Company. This project is partially funded by a grant from the E.N.H.C., the Saugus Business Partnership, and the Saugus Theatre Company.

This week workers are updating the buildings electrical system and installing a dedicated circuit for a new gas burner. National Grid has recently completed the installation of a pipeline from the street to school. Although the building had to be closed for the winter due to lack of heat, the Foundation is pleased with the feedback they have received from a benevolent organization willing to fund the heating project.

Mr. Joseph Gould, A G.E. representative of the G.E. Good Neighbor Fund, toured the building with his staff saw the need and recognized the potential. The Fund awarded $50,000.00 to replace the antiquated oil burner and convert to gas heat. The completion of this phase allowed us to now keep the building open all year.

Additional good fortune came when the V.F.W. offered to supply the Foundation with tables and chairs from their Main Street headquarters which was in the process of closing their doors temporarily. The banquet size tables and chairs will allow the MEG Foundation to rent rooms in the building for small parties, showers, and collations after funerals. Good news also came for Ron and Janice Long this week who have agreed to donate a piano and refrigerator to the MEG Foundation.

The Foundation is going "Green" with efforts to update the electrical system, and the installation of energy efficient light bulbs. In addition, new Low-E insulated window replacements will soon be installed in the basement and on the first-floor level. The use of solar panels and/or wind power to produce electricity for the building is also being considered. The Foundation anticipates applying for a grant for this and other energy saving projects in the future. By going green the Foundation will maintain a healthy building for the public that is environmentally responsible and cost-efficient. The Foundation's goal is to create a center of culture, education, and civic pride for the entire community within this historic building.

The MEG Foundation has applied for a grant from the Massachusetts Cultural Council to completely restore the original slate roof of the school that dates to 1894 when the school was built. Michael Doane of Stanley Roofing Company will direct and supervise the slate roof restoration and repair work. Ironically, Michael is a descendent of the original architect, Penn Varney of Lynn who designed the school in 1894 for Charles Bond and the Town of Saugus. The relation is on his mother's side and he is the great, great, great grandson of Mr. Varney.

Penn Varney was born on Nov. 15, 1859 in Wolfeboro, N. H. and came to Lynn in 1882 to learn architectural drafting with H. K. Wheeler. In 1888 he established his own business and became a very successful architect. He designed Classical High School and the Essex Trust Company building on 35 Exchange Street in Lynn. Locally, he designed the Melrose Public Library, the Winthrop Theatre, and the Gardner Memorial Building and Town Hall. His work can also be seen out of state as follows; Schenectady, N.Y.- the public library, the Gleason building, the Brown building, the Vendome Hotel and the private residence of H.S. De Forest and in Amsterdam, N.Y. the Elks' Home.

In Portland, Maine - the Porteous Mitchell and Braun building; in Sacco, Maine - the Biddeford Institute of Savings, in Sanford, Maine – the Town Hall and in Skowhegan, Maine - the First National Bank Building. Lastly, he designed the public library in Barre, Vermont.

The original blueprints designed by Penn Varney in 1893 for the Bond School were extremely difficult to locate but necessary for the restoration. Months were spent in various departments in Saugus and Lynn to find the blueprints with no luck. Finally, through the efforts of a friend and historian in Lynn, the original blueprints were found at the State Archives in Boston.

All these efforts would not be possible without the help and support of many Saugonians near and far and board members of the MEG Foundation. We look with great anticipation on the upcoming improvements and continued restoration of the Marleah E. Graves Building.

Our Mission Statement

Our Mission

Why a Cultural Center in Saugus?

In the late 1800's the land for the Cliftondale School was made available to the town by Mr. Charles H. Bond, a resident of the Cliftondale area of Saugus. Mr. Bond was a very generous benefactor of public education and the arts.

In 1894, the Cliftondale School was built by the Town of Saugus and designed by Penn Varney of Lynn, Massachusetts. Mr. Varney also designed libraries in Vermont and Woburn, Massachusetts, to name a few.

Inherent in the aesthetics of this building's design is an essential beauty and structural soundness, which makes it a candidate to be one of the most significant structures in Saugus.

In order to begin this process, we welcome contributions from those who have an interest in promoting civic awareness and culture in the Saugus area, along with financial assistance from benevolent businesses, corporations, banks, and all organizations which have within their charter a spirit of charity for the community of which they are a part.

The Cliftondale School Study Committee, which first formed in May of 2006, has focused on the restoration of Marleah Grave's second grade classroom in the first step of a long range plan to utilize this building for the benefit of the community. Miss Graves was a very popular and much loved teacher in the Cliftondale School for close to 50 years.

We look forward to providing facilities to the community and envision the Marleah Graves Cultural Center to eventually become a magnet for artists, thespians, literary groups, and local community organizations.

Early friends of the MEG

Agganis, Peter and Family	Andrews Family
Armstrong, Donald	Attubato Family
Austill, Stephen and Virginia	Bogdan Family
Bond Family	Ciccarelli Family
Danversbank – David Fama	DiNardo, Al
Dolan, Richard and Justine	Eastern Bank- Linda Pogson
Essex National Heritage	GCA Jewelers, Greg Chiulli
GE Good Neighbor Fund	Geriatric Assistance
Gould, Dennis, GE	Hewitt, Paul
Jarosz, Eric, Ron, Dan, Dave	Jarosz, Jay, Jay T. Amber
Jarosz, Tom, Jessica, Tommy	Kowalsky Family
Lowe's	Ludwig Family
Materese, Ralph	Merrithew, Barbara
Mugar, David	Mugar, Carolyn
Nickole Leo	Nigro, James
North Shore Bank	Parker, Lisa, Haley, Andrew
Penney Construction, Ryan Penney	Procopio Enterprises
Rossetti Family	Sarver, Dolores
Saugus Business Partnership	Saugus Federal Credit Union, John Smolinsky
Saugus Garden Club	Saugus Inspectional Services
Saugus Police Patrol Officers Union	Saugus Youth and Recreation
Simpson, George	Sola, Rose Marie
Taylor, Marianne	Theater Company of Saugus
Wheelabrator, John O'Rourke	Wong, Donald Kowloon

Volunteers come to the rescue

Whoever said "Many the hands make light the work" must have known about those wonderful citizens who dedicated many long hours in the restoration. Board members, town officials, friends, and families, so many supporters and workers contributed, not only physical labor, but moral support as well!

Former School Department Member Gene Leighton took charge of removing the old windows. He stated on one visit, "I served in the School Department for 37 years and had many occasions to meet with Miss Graves. She was a much-loved teacher by not only the children, but by her colleagues as well."

Saugonian Jack Curry – Former School Committee member and former President of Northeastern University offered his help along with Peter and Shirley Bogdan, Mike Serino, Clayton and Helen Trefry.

Ever since the beginning of the school's 're-birth,' Mr. Al DiNardo, owner of DiNardo Landscaping of Saugus, continues to this day to care for our lawn and landscaping needs. The MEG is also blessed to have two guardian angels devoted to the care and protection of the MEG. John and Kathy Giannetta consider the MEG their 'home away from home.' They visit just about day making sure everything is in order. John does all the necessary maintenance, fixes anything that's broken, refinishes woodwork, and serves as 'chief cook and bottle washer.' Kathy oversees the schedule of events, orders supplies, washes and waxes everything in sight and if there is one speck of dust, she will find it. Their dedication to the MEG is priceless!

MEG and Saugus Cable TV meet

Lights, camera, action!

Community television president wants to start up local station

SAUGUS

By CHRIS STEVENS
THE DAILY ITEM

Saugus Community Television President Joe Kennedy has a challenge for the people who live and work in Saugus.

"I want your ideas, your creativity, your thoughts," he said. "I have a big old soap box and there's plenty of room."

When the federal government announced that cable companies could get out of the local station business, the town found itself scrambling to figure out how to run a cable station.

Then came Joe Kennedy. Kennedy has been on disability for more than one year, the result of major heart surgery that included the replacement of two valves, which stemmed from a bout of cancer when he was 11.

"I've always told myself I wanted to do something community-based but really effective," he said.

And the cable station fit that bill.

With Jim Wlodyka, who has six years experience working with Comcast, as his right hand man, Kennedy has set an aggressive timetable to get the station up and on the air.

"We have an operational studio at the high school," he said, "and we'll use that for now."

Kennedy, however, is cautiously optimistic in regards to long term plans that with a little luck could have him moving to the second floor of the Marleah Graves School.

Walking through the old classrooms, Kennedy kicks flaked paint chips aside and sidesteps pigeon droppings as he explains his vision.

He sees the old principal's office as eventually the executive director's digs, one large classroom as a common working area and additional rooms as a control office and studio.

He points to one of the small cloak rooms that sit at the entrance of each classroom and said he'd like to turn it into a small green room for people waiting for studio time.

All that potential is currently speculation, however, until a lease is worked out with the Marleah Graves Foundation.

What isn't mere speculation, he insists, is his vision for the station wherever it lands.

Kennedy wants to keep a working relationship with the schools and with Youth and Recreation Director Greg Nickolas on the cable board and also hopes to reach out to middle schoolers and troubled youths.

"There are a lot of troubled kids with lots to say," he said, "and we'll give them a voice."

Kennedy is also hoping to turn channel 10, the school's educational station into an educational station for everyone. Channel eight will remain the local government/public access station but again Kennedy said he is hoping to grow the station's offerings.

Along with airing various board and committee meetings, Kennedy said he'd like to have town officials come onto the show to break down what happens at the meeting for everyday citizens.

"I think a big problem in town is there is so little education leading up to various issues," he said. "People have little understanding."

Kennedy said he believes that if officials took the time to clue residents in on why things were happening and how issues will be addressed more people would get involved or at least be accepting of changes.

He also pointed out that the station is not controlled by the town or Comcast so anyone with an opposing viewpoint is also welcome to air their opinions.

In fact, Kennedy is hoping about disabled residents.

"I want a mix of everything," he said. "We've bantered around doing a live music show on Friday nights. We'd have a little coffee house and show live musicians."

He's also looking at what other communities are doing for programming to get ideas such as Malden's Able Vision, a show run by disabled residents.

Joe Kennedy and Jim Wlodyka sitting at the board room table in the community room.

"I would look for people in Saugus who would like to have their stories shown," he said. "I would like to show anything anyone might have an interest in."

Kennedy admits his ambitions are big but said he has one thing working in his favor.

"No one is against us," he said. "It's not like there is some big competing cable company saying we want that too. It's great. And it will not cost the town one dime."

His target date is to have the station fully operational by January with new programming running by March.

Kennedy said he would encourage anyone with a flare for dramatics or a passion for the technical side of things to stop by the studio.

"We would love to hear from you," he said.

There will be a membership contract to those that want to use a camera and volunteers will have to be trained but Kennedy encourages anyone to stop by and see him during Founders Day, they'll be in front of Town Hall for more information.

(Saugus Advertiser)

It was a chance meeting that the late Joseph Kennedy and several board members met. Mr. Kennedy was adamant that he did not want to move into the high school as the location was isolated – and a far cry from the original studio on Jackson Street.

The cable studio moved into the building on the first floor and the board attempted to get heat into the building to make a permanent home for our new tennant. Unfortunately, the directors were unable to secure a promise for year round use and Mr. Kennedy was left with the choice of moving into the high school.

Our First Gathering!!

The newly elected board members of the MEG Foundation hosted an open house on Wednesday, October 22, 2008 at the Marleah Graves School, formerly known as the Cliftondale School. Friends and neighbors were invited to tour the building and view the progress made in two classrooms on the first floor.

The late Mr. Don Armstrong and Mary Ann Taylor, Directors of the MEG Foundation, were chairmen of the event and served as official greeters. Other members on the committee were Marilyn Carlson, Ruth Swanson, and Helen Holt, who also donated homemade ginger cookies; Cam Cicolini also contributed a tray of her special desserts and MEG Board Member, John Smolinsky served as M.C.

Musical Director Ms. Nancy Lemoine

(Photo JKJ, courtesy of Lemoine family)

Ms. Nancy Lemoine, Music Director at Saugus High School, led the Saugus High School Girls Quartet with several popular songs entertaining the audience to the enjoyment of all. An Art Exhibit was presented as well from students from Saugus High School.

Many families, friends and organizations contributed to the success of the event; Ms. Lee Dyment, and Donna Manoogian of the Saugus Garden Club designed beautiful fall floral arrangements which graced the building and served as raffle prizes; Ms. Jean Lobbregt assisted in decorating the classrooms and Janice Williamson baked scores of homemade goodies. Ms. Margie Berkowitch, of Saugus Quilters Guild, donated a handmade quilt which was raffled off at the second fundraiser on Wednesday, October 29, 2008.

Dunkin Donuts of Cliftondale donated hot coffee with all the fixings and Lena's Subs contributed a platter of sandwiches and enjoyed by all.

Mr. Leo Nicole, of the Theater Company of Saugus, displayed various memorabilia of the organization and served as host to the Open House.

Members of the MEG Foundation extended their deepest appreciation to those attended the event and all who continue to support the ever-challenging restoration of the Marleah E. Graves School.

Our First Fundraiser!!

Saugus Selectmen and town officials put on a show!!

Selectmen Steve Castinetti Mike Kelleher, Fire Chief Jim Blanchard, Chris Blanchard, Selectmen Donald Wong, Peter Rossetti and Steve Horlick; Attorney Arthur Gustafson, and Master of Ceremonies and MEG board member John Smolinsky.

(JKJ)

Talented cast members of The Theatre Company of Saugus joined forces with somewhat less musically inclined town officials on March 13, 2008 to delight fellow Saugonians by performing a slate of popular Broadway show tunes.

The MEG Foundation and Theatre Company of Saugus jointly presented 'From Broadway to Hollywood,' a musical production conceived of and directed by Leo Nickole featuring nearly two dozen songs that opened on Broadway. The VFW Hall was packed with fans to witness the talent and hear music of famous songs.

Our Patriotic leaders of Saugus, MA

Jkj

The entire company appeared on stage for the first act and busted into, "There's no business-like show business." Performing were Fire Chief James Blanchard and his wife Chris, Charlie and Lois Thomas, Peter and Shirley Bogdan, Jackie Howard, Arthur Gustafson and Selectmen Donald Wong, Michael Kelleher, Stephen Horlick, Stephan Castinetti and Peter Rossetti, Jr. Audience members clapped their hands and tapped their toes while they sang along throughout the night from "Lullaby of Broadway" to the patriotic closing of "You're a Grand Old Flag."

All five selectmen donned green hats and glittery bows to sing, 'When Irish Eyes are smiling' then honored the request when the charmed audience pleaded for an encore.

Selectman Kelleher commented, "The board must not have been too bad at singing as the audience wanted to hear more! I think everyone had a great time which is the most important thing."

Restored entranceway

MEG Board Member Kathryn Hollett, an interior designer, took it upon herself to restore the lobby back to its original beauty with new floors, lighting, and paint. Later Ms. Hollett purchased two oriental rugs and a hospitality bar to complete the final touches!

(jkj)

McCormick Kitchens – Saugus, MA

(jkj)

I visited McCormick Kitchens several years ago requesting advice and asking if someone could visit the MEG to view our building. The timing was perfect as a representative asked if I wanted the floor model that was about to be removed. One thing led to another and, before long, a brand new, fully equipped, state of the art kitchen with cabinets, counter tops, refrigerator, stove, micro range, garbage disposal and sink all donated by McCormack Kitchens of Saugus, MA.

We at the MEG are eternally grateful to McCormick Kitchens!

The Wellness Center

(jkj)

The second-floor classroom renovation sponsored by Doreen Correnti, of Geriatric Assistance, Inc., in memory of her late sister.

Geriatric Assistance Team

Patty Cashman, Doreen Correnti, Sue Rollfs, and John Macauda. Both Doreen Correnti and John Macauda are MEG Board Members.

(JKJ)

Brand New hardwood floor in the MEG room

MEG board member Ruth Swanson sponsored new hardwood flooring for the MEG classroom and it now can entertain dancing groups and classes.

(jkj)

Charles Henry Bond comes home

Ralph Matarese, Al Faragi, and Marilyn Carlson.

(jkj)

Chapter VI

MEMORIES OF THE CLIFTONDALE SCHOOL 1976-1978

By Debbie Alcott Nickolas

Our favorite lunch aide was Mrs. Driscoll. She lived in Saugus on Essex Street which was not too far from the school. Our school always had the big bell that rang.

The most popular game we played during physical education class was "Capture the Flag." We would all go down the fire escape to play this game in the school yard.

We stored all of our lunches and coats in the coatroom corals that were built outside the classrooms.

I remember Mrs. Anne Wilson who was our first-grade teacher. She loved teaching us about nature. Her husband would often visit our classroom and show us slides of butterflies.

Miss Marleah Graves retired the year before our class entered second grade and Mrs. Peppy took her place.

Mr. Bruce Waybright was one of the most memorable and creative teachers I ever had at the Cliftondale School. I can still remember many of the fun things we did in his classroom. There were square-dancing, cultural lessons, plays, outdoor activities, clean-up, contests and games down at Anna Parker Playground.

The Cliftondale School always held outdoor Memorial Day Programs.

During my four years at the school, the class size was very small which enabled us to become very close to one another.

Photo of Classmates

Debbie Alcott Nicholas

Mr. Waybright's 1978 class

The fourth grade class of teacher, Bruce Waybright in 1978 included (Top row, l to r): Kevin McCabe, Mike Merrit, Scott Slattery, Mike Olsen, Kevin Andrews; Middle Row: Darren Caninia, Dennis McLennan, Kevin Littlefield, Bob Blaney and Lance Nichols; and Front Row: Marria Villagraica, Jonna Gillis, Eileen Olsen, Debbie Moore, Debbie Alcott and Kathy Dwyer.

Fourth grade class reunited in 2006

Pictured at the December 2006 reunion 28 years after they graduated from fourth grade are Top Row (l to r): Michael Olsen, Kevin Andrews, Michael Merrit, Dennis Mclennan; Middle Row: Jonna Gillis Moses, empty chair, Debbie (Alcott) Nickolas, Debbie (Moore) Miller, Kathy Dwyer and Marria (Villagracia) Brown; and Front Row: Lance Nichols, Darren Caginia, Bobby Blany, Timmy Millea and Kevin McCabe.

(Courtesy of Saugus Advertiser)

Kentucky Derby Fundraiser 2014

Front row: Lee Dyment, Ruth Swanson, Mary Ann Taylor, Janice Jarosz, Charlotte Line, Joseph Anannian, Chickie Holllett and Jean Solious.

The MEG held its' first Kentucky Derby replete with fashonable dresses and hats and topped off with the best Mint Julips this side of the Rio Grande!!

(Courtesy of Saugus Advertiser)

Saugus High School Alumni Association

Front Row: Cam Cicolini, Librarian Kate Payne, Rheta (Tia) Kramer, Judy Alabisio and Charlotte Line

Back Row: Janice Jarosz, Phyllis Anthony, Julie Piercey, and Rick LaVoie, Teacher.

MEG Annual Christmas Tree Festival

Several years ago, board member Charlotte Line suggested the MEG host a Christmas Tree Festival as a fundraiser and her idea became a yearly event! The festival has grown into one of the most successful and joyful events of the season.

(jkj)

Andrews Family Toy Drive   Kathy - the resident elf

(jkj)

The MEG hosted meetings for the Saugus Military Families, Saugus Rotary art shows, Belmonte Middle School annual concerts; Saugus Girl Scouts Foster Care Project; Mark Andrews yearly Haunted House; Kevin Andrews Toy Drive, Dan Jarosz Sneaker Convention and Charlotte Line's Cursive Writing classes.

Santa Eric with helpers David and Tommy

(jkj)

Troop 62 Congregational Church Boy Scouts

(jkj)

Troop 62 from the Cliftondale Congregrational Church offers help each year with the Christmas Festival and many other chores around the building. Santa vists, hot cocoa and cookies are served and Christmas music echoes thoughout the building. Dozens of beautiful Christmas trees are displayed with individual themes. Drawing of raffle tickets culminates the closing of the festival. The Festival is a joyous occasion each year!!!

New Hope Assembly of God Nativity Scene

(jkj)

The MEG Foundation Activities

The Marleah Elizabeth Graves (MEG) Foundation is administered by a volunteer board of directors committed to restoring this historic building for cultural events and community organizations – activities enriching all of our lives. Funding for the MEG Foundation is provided by individual donations, benevolent business contributions, and grants. Board members volunteer their time and energy and are committed to the preservation of this maginficant building for all to enjoy.

The Foundation has hosted many other special events including the following:

Art Exhibits featuring professional artists – Donald Mosher, Tom Sutherland, Bill Maloney and Jeff Fioravanti. The History of the Theater siminars by Mr. Leo Nickole, Emeritus Professor at Emerson College, the American Musical Theatre's Golden Age, Realism of the Art of Theatre, and The Principles of Play Directing. Our first fundraiser, A Musical Review by the Theatre Company of Saugus and community champions entited 'From Broadway to Hollywood' performed at the VFW.

A Retrospective Exhibit featuring the creative works of many Saugus art teachers over the years directed by Mr. Michael Donovan: The Art Teachers of Saugus: Past, Present, and Future. Vocal Performances by the Saugus High School students directed by Nancy Lemoine: Girls Acappella Choir and KAMA & the Tune Squad. Musical Performances by Saugus High School students directed by Amanda Shelly several years ago featuring a Saxophone Quartet and Jazz Band. Belmonte concerts, also under the direction of Amanda Shelly, are very popular and well attended each spring.

A Literary Tribute to Mr. John Burns arranged by Mr. Tom Sheehan and Mr. Bob Wentworth (Millennium Book Committee) A celebration of the lilfe of former teacher John Burns in prose and poetry. A Evening of Classical Music performd by the Rosewood String Trio of Wakefield at the Donor's Appreciation Night, Slightly Off Broadway Production Company with co-owners Brittany Daley and Laura Liberge presented "The Complete Works of William Shakespeare" and "Annabel's" a play of the macabre taken from a poem by Edgar Allen Poe.

Our volunteers and board members have been very busy these past 10 years! The MEG hosted dozens of showers for brides and mothers to be; nonprofit events in support of cancer research, and several other health fundraising efforts; birthday parties for young and the not so young; Girl Scout events, a Sneaker Convention, Daughters of the American Revolution, and Saugus Chamber of Commerce meetings.

The MEG is also headquarters for American and National Little League, Pop Warner and cheerleader signups, coaches' meetings, private grief, AA meetings, and funeral collations.

Chapter VII

MEG Foundation celebrates 10 years!!!

Cathryn and Carla Hollett, Artists

On October 2, 2017, a celebration was held at the Marleah Elizabeth Graves (MEG) school in appreciation to those who accomplished the almost impossible. Today the former and once forgotten school building is 'alive and well' because of so many dedicated board members, friends and families who contributed endless time, energy, and talents to provide a place for all to enjoy.

The Celebration opened with Miss Alicia Felix singing the National Anthem followed by MEG Board Member, Mr. John Smolinsky, serving as Master of Ceremonies. Mr. Smolinsky was one of the first businessman in the community to recognize the potential of renovating the former Cliftondale School. His generous support in the early and tenuous times, gave the rest of us much of the spirit and fortitude to move forward.

Entertainment was provided by New Hope Assembly of God musicians and memorial plaques were given to those in attendance.

Master of Ceremonies John Smolinsky

(Steve Bevacqua Photographer)

New Hope Assembly of God Musicians

Ashley Shirk, Jasmine Pina, Elijah Aboidor, Joshua Jean Charles and Matthew White

(Steve Bevacqua Photographer)

Marleah E. Graves (MEG) Board of Directors
2007 - 2017

Back Row: John Giannetta, Bill McAdoo, John Smolinsky, and John Macauda, Middle Row: Denise Selden, Charlotte Line, Paula Walsh, Linda Ross, Kathryn Hollett, and Linda Tonnegrossa. Front Row: Kathy Giannetta, Janice Jarosz, Lee Dyment, and Ruth Swanson.

(Steve Bevacqua Photographer)

Marleah E. Graves (MEG) Board of Directors
2007 – 2020

*Donald Armstrong
*Charles D. Bond
Marilyn Carlson
Cam Cicolini
Doreen Correnti

Lee Dyment
*Anthony (Tony) Eovine
Donna Federico
Kathy Giannetta
John Giannetta
Phoebe Hernandez
Kathryn (Chickie) Hollett
Helen Holt
Janice Jarosz
Michael LaVecchia
Charlotte (Carly) Line
William (Bill) McAdoo
John Macauda
Linda Ross
Joyce Rossetti
John Smolinsky
Jean Solious
Anthony (Tony) Speziale
Patty Staples
Ruth Stead
*Mary Ann Taylor
Lynda Tonnegrossa
Paula Walsh

*deceased

Looking toward the future

By Janice K. Jarosz

As Saugus is widely recognized as the gate way to the North Shore, we are looking to the future and hoping to develop a Visitor's Center at the MEG. Our vision is to serve as a welcoming center to visitors and provide information, brochures, maps, historical places to visit, recommendations on what to see, and what to do while visiting our beautiful Saugus and surrounding areas.

Another proposal on the table to bring back 'Merchant's Row' an event that took place in the 70's - blocking off Lincoln Avenue and featuring all the businesses and highlighting the food establishments and opportunities. Back in the 70's merchants put their wares out on the sidewalks; a live band was stationed on the Rotary and parking lots were filled with fun and games for the younger set.

A perennial issue we hope to resolve in the short future is the challenge of converting the MEG building into handicap accessibility status. We have been working on this for many years and, hopefully, we may be able to install a lift soon.

We welcome all residents to visit the MEG to see firsthand what many of our citizens, town officials and businesses contributed to provide this beautiful building for all of us to treasure and enjoy! Today the beautiful MEG building stands as a shining example of what can be accomplished when we all work together.

I extend my deepest appreciation to the late Charles Henry Bond and for all who contributed to the rebuilding and preservation of this proud landmark we share in our town today. So close to that wrecking ball, the citizens of Saugus stood up, prevented the proposed demolition, and saved the beautiful MEG for generations to come. I applaud you all.

"Many hands make light the work and, if you will call your troubles experiences and remember that every experience develops some latent force within you, you will grow vigorous and happy, however adverse your circumstances may seem to be."

John Heywood

(English Playwright and Poet, 1497-1580)

Charles Henry Bond looking down fondly at his grandsons celebrating the first gathering of the residents of Saugus in 2007 at the Bond/MEG School.

Left to right: Zot and Allen Bond, Janice Jarosz, and Charles D. Bond